OAKWOOD REMINISCENCE SERIES

Hillhoı Immortals

The story of a
London & North Western Railway
Engine Shed and its men

by
Neil Fraser

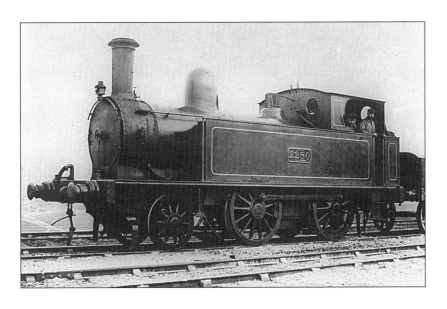

THE OAKWOOD PRESS

© Oakwood Press & Neil Fraser 1999

British Library Cataloguing in Publication Data
A Record for this book is available from the British Library
ISBN 0 85361 548 9

Typeset by Oakwood Graphics.
Repro by Ford Graphics, Ringwood, Hants.
Printed by Cambrian Printers, Aberystwyth, Ceredigion.

Frank Knight, steamraiser with fire shovel, laden with fire, on his shoulder.

Revd R.G. Johnson

Title page: LNWR 'Chopper' tank No. 2280 used on the Birstal branch.

Author's Collection

Published by The Oakwood Press (Usk), P.O. Box 13, Usk, Mon., NP15 1YS.
E-Mail: oakwood-press@dial.pipex.com
Website: http://ds.dial.pipex.com/oakwood-press

Contents

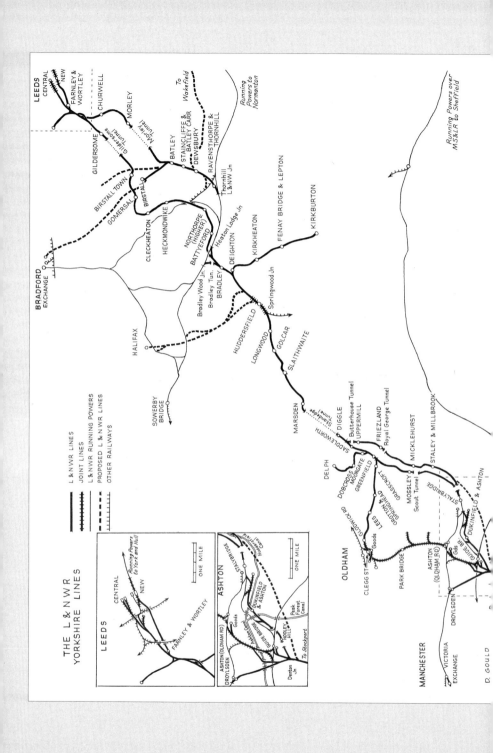

THE L & N W R
YORKSHIRE LINES

L & N W R LINES
JOINT LINES
L & N W R RUNNING POWERS
PROPOSED L & N W R LINES
OTHER RAILWAYS

LEEDS

CENTRAL
NEW
FARNLEY & WORTLEY
Running Powers to York and Hull
ONE MILE

ASHTON

ASHTON (OLDHAM RD)
DROYLSDEN
Goods
STALYBRIDGE
DUKINFIELD & ASHTON
BRADLEY HILL
GUIDE BRIDGE
Peak Forest Canal
To Stockport
Denton Jn
ONE MILE

LEEDS

CENTRAL
NEW
FARNLEY & WORTLEY
CHURWELL
MORLEY
Morley Tunnel
Gildersome Tunnel
GILDERSOME
BIRSTALL TOWN
GOMERSAL
BIRSTALL
BATLEY
STAINCLIFFE & BATLEY CARR
DEWSBURY
To Wakefield
RAVENSTHORPE & THORNHILL
Thornhill L & NW Jn
Running Powers to Normanton

BRADFORD
EXCHANGE
CLECKHEATON
HECKMONDWIKE
NORTHORPE (HIGHER)
BATTYEFORD
Bradley Wood Jn.
Bradley Tun.
BRADLEY
Heaton Lodge Jn
DEIGHTON
KIRKHEATON
FENAY BRIDGE & LEPTON
KIRKBURTON
Springwood Jn
HUDDERSFIELD
HALIFAX
LONGWOOD
GOLCAR
SLAITHWAITE
SOWERBY BRIDGE
MARSDEN
Standedge Tunnel
SADDLEWORTH
DIGGLE
Butterhouse Tunnel
UPPERMILL
DELPH
DOBCROSS
MOORGATE
GREENFIELD
FRIEZLAND
Royal George Tunnel
GRASSCROFT
GROTTON SPRINGHEAD
LEES
MOSSLEY
Scout Tunnel
MICKLEHURST
STALEY & MILLBROOK
STALYBRIDGE
DUKINFIELD & ASHTON

Running Powers over MS&LR to Sheffield

OLDHAM
GLODWICK RD
CLEGG ST
Goods
PARK BRIDGE
ASHTON (OLDHAM RD)
GUIDE BR
DROYLSDEN

MANCHESTER
VICTORIA
EXCHANGE

D. GOULD

Foreword

Some of this material was presented in talks given 1962-1965 to the Stephenson Locomotive Society and the Railway Correspondence and Travel Society, while extracts have been published in the *Huddersfield Examiner*, *SLS Journal*, *Premier News* and *LNWR Journal*.

The author is glad to acknowledge the help received from Ian Fraser, Geoff Brown, who prepared the map and diagram, David Gledhill, B.S. Norman also the late Harry Eastwood, Curtis Elsworth, Bill Elson, Harry Gatenby, Claude Langton, Charlie Smith, Albert Mortimer, Walter Woods and C. Williams, the late Kenneth Field, J.E. Hirst and Mrs S. Schofield (daughter of James Goulding). Of the photographers, the late Revd Richard Garrett Johnson, Vicar of St Andrews, Hillhouse 1903-1909 was a friend of the Goulding family. P.F. Cooke in the period 1919-1929 had the contents of Hillhouse Shed drawn out for his benefit on many Sunday mornings. In that same age Cyril Whitaker took many action shots, while George Taylor Rhodes (1860-1922) was credited with many photographs down the ages, although many of these were taken by others, but which formed the background to his lantern lectures on 'Our Railways' given in many church halls and Sunday Schools from 1882 onwards.

To set the scene. I am often reminded of an old friend, who when his engine passed Canker Lane, would eject a well aimed shovel of coal between cab and tender down an embankment. By this means a nearby greenhouse was kept heated every winter for almost 40 years!

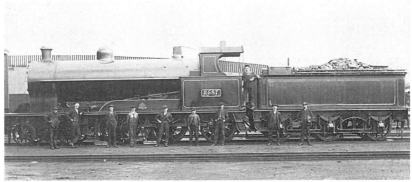

Hillhouse 19 in. 4-6-0 No. 2587 was used as pilot engine for Royal Train empty stock in 1918. From left, (2) Arthur Harris, fitter; (4) Leonard Crosland, boilersmith; (5) Vincent Boyle; (6) John Hughes; (7) Arnold Davis, joint maker; (9) Joe Noden, fitter.

Author's Collection

Preface

London and North Western: a name that excites the imagination and charged the atmosphere with great achievements in the realm of railway enterprise. One of the London and North Western's (LNWR) less fashionable engine sheds forms the background to this work, a shed where there were no household names and few famous engines - its stud being drawn from a worthy assortment of hard slogging dividend earners. Situated half a mile north of Huddersfield on the Manchester-Leeds route, Hillhouse Shed was animated by highly contrasting figures possessed of many good human qualities, and a few with a share of human failings. Men whose words and humour deserve recall and whose stirring deeds quickens the blood.

Remembrance of past generations of men and engines is tempered by the fact that of all the characteristics with which humans are endowed, it is often by some particular incident that they are remembered.

I hope I have been able to convey some of the pleasure I experienced in gathering this material from those who left their own indelible mark in railway history.

I come from a background which included a grandfather who was an LNWR driver but who died when I was but three months old, leaving behind a large family and diaries spanning the period 1896-1917. I would like to acknowledge the courteous help and assistance received from many friends and acquaintances at the former Hillhouse Shed, who with much patience answered countless searching questions.

Coal Tank No. 2483 on the Kirkburton motor train at Huddersfield in the charge of driver Harry Tuckfield. This locomotive was allocated to Hillhouse between 1925 and 1927.

P.F. Cooke

Introduction

The presence of a locomotive at Huddersfield was indicated in a minute of the Huddersfield and Manchester Railway and Canal Company recording the delivery of an engine in March 1847. As the viaduct approach to the station was not then complete it may be assumed that the engine came no nearer than Hillhouse, a reference to an engine shed there is contained in the *Leeds Mercury* of 30th October of the same year, when it was noted that such premises were under construction and was sometimes referred to as the Whitestone Engine shed, Sugdens Fields. This building comprised four roads and four E.B. Wilson 0-6-0s ordered by the Leeds, Dewsbury and Manchester railway were in store there in March 'as no use could be found for them at the present time'. The volume of work increased when the route to Manchester as opened in 1849.

By 1867 there were five engines at Hillhouse and the four roads were divided, two for engines, one for coal storage and spare engines while the fourth was reserved for the wagon department. Accommodation was provided for 20 engines, and this remained unchanged until 1878 when plans to enlarge the premises to accommodate 24 engines were completed in April 1881.

Between March 1906 and April 1907 the shed was reconstructed to its ultimate size, the section used by the wagon department having been vacated in November 1905 and part subsequently demolished. The shed also became a through building at this time.

Landmarks in the years that followed include the disbandment of the breakdown gang in 1932; the fitting of a new roof in 1935 and the construction of an automatic coaling and ash disposal plant in 1936. The wheel drop remained until 1937 but was damaged when run into by an engine, and never repaired.

Under the mid-1950s Scheme for the Modernisation of the Railways the shed was earmarked to stable diesel multiple units and Nos. 7, 8 and 9 roads were to be partitioned off for that purpose with fuel tanks erected in the roof, but this never materialised. Threatened with closure during the summer of 1963, the shed lingered on until 2nd January, 1967 when its steam allocation was dispersed, becoming a signing-on point for crews manning main line diesel locomotives allocated to Healey Mills depot, until complete closure came on 5th November, 1967.

The LNWR shed code was 20 carried on a white enamel plate with black figures and placed at the back of a locomotive's cab roof. In February 1931 this was changed to C7, the shed since 1928 being in the LMS Railway's Central Division. The position of the shed plate had also been altered to the foot of the smokebox door. In October 1934 it was changed again to 25B and remained so until altered to 55G on 26th January, 1957 - shed plates actually being changed on 4th June of that year.

The first significant duty became evident during 1849 when a pilot engine was assigned to assist all trains through the 3 miles and 62 yards-long single line Standedge tunnel. The growth of traffic and delays caused awaiting the pilot's return resulted in criticism from many quarters.

On 6th April, 1850 one of its drivers, Michael Kelley, was found drunk on duty and unable to mount the footplate. Consequently he served six months at the Wakefield House of Corrrection.

On 3rd November, 1852, the pilot, one of the original Manchester and Birmingham Railway's Sharp Singles built in the early 1840s, which finished their lives on the Yorkshire lines, suffered a failure of its crank axle as it was

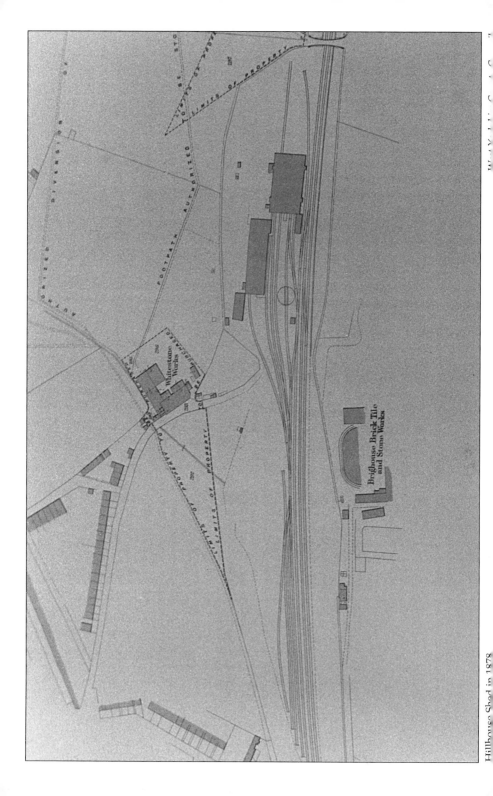

Hillhouse Shed in 1878.

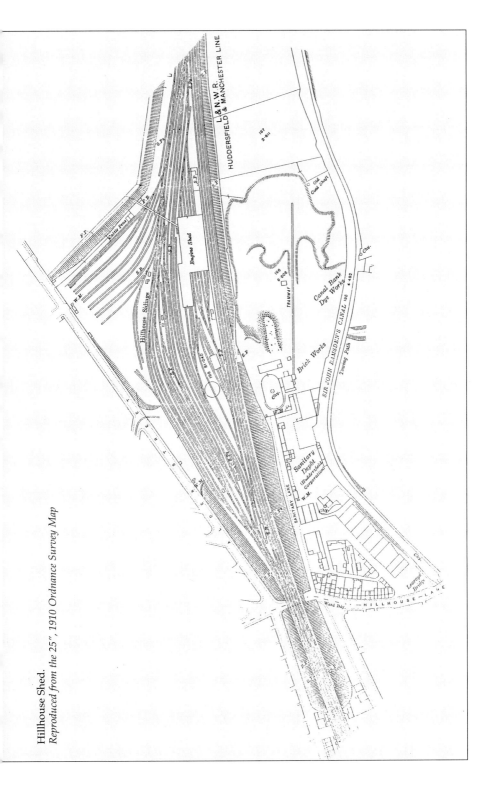

Hillhouse Shed.
Reproduced from the 25″, 1910 Ordnance Survey Map

piloting the 5 pm Manchester-Leeds express, the *Huddersfield Chronicle* observing: 'This poor and aged machine is in a sad way. It is monstrous that a wealthy company like the LNWR should allow a machine which is afflicted with all the ills that old engines are heir to, to be used'. It later became the practice to allow a series of trains through in one direction, the pilot being attached to the last one. Needless to say mishaps occurred with this altered arrangement, but it did expedite matters better than before.

Thomas Norman at Crewe on 27th November, 1893, locomotive foreman at Hillhouse Shed from 1882 to 1894. He died in Oldham in 1909.   *LNWR Society*

Chapter One

Top People

In 1847 Hillhouse Shed was in charge of a Mr Roche (some newspapers of the day refer to Mr Rhodes). Designated locomotive superintendent, he was privileged to drive the Sharp Single *Aldam* on its inaugural journey from Huddersfield to Heaton Lodge on 2nd August, 1847. Successors were styled locomotive foremen and all earned fame for their proficiency in organising breakdown operations following accidents and mishaps. During the period 1850-1900 these amounted to no fewer than 163 cases involving LNWR trains on the lines east of Stalybridge.

The tenure of Thomas Norman, who commenced work at the shed in 1855, was notable in that the entire route between Heaton Lodge Jn to Stalybridge was quadrupled with a corresponding increase in the shed's duties. Norman was born at Glynde in Sussex and his first experience of steam was aboard early Channel paddle steamers. He joined the LNWR at Camden in 1847, moving from there to Copley Hill in 1852.

The Yorkshire Lines were not often used by Royal travellers, but on 13th October, 1882 the Duke and Duchess of Albany journeyed from Otley to Huddersfield. The train was hauled by 6 ft 6 in. 'Precedent' No. 857 *Prince Leopold* driven by George Mossley, a very placid man, who on this occasion, due to an exchange of words with G.E. Mawby the district superintendent, misjudging his braking resulting in the train overshooting the appointed stopping place and having to set back to where the red carpet was laid. (The event was repeated on 14th October, 1971 upon arrival of HM The Queen.)

Thomas Norman was succeeded in 1894 by a striking figure, James Goulding, regarded by some with the same esteem traditionally reserved for Regimental Sergeant Majors. At times it could be a scorching experience to be within earshot when he gave relief to his feelings, and if there is any truth in the adage that cleanliness is next to godliness, then Hillhouse must have been a Holy place! But his ability was demonstrated shortly after his arrival when two accidents occurred at Mirfield. Until quadrupling in 1932 all trains converged onto two lines over the Calder; a down loop by the station afforded slight relief, and beyond Cleckheaton Jn (later Mirfield No. 3) the lines opened out again to four tracks. On the night of 28th March, 1895 'Special DX' No. 1580 on a Leeds goods was detained in the loop, but the driver appeared to have overlooked this, and seeing an 'off' signal (for the main line), applied steam and ran through the buffers, the engine and train plunging down the banking and finishing in a sea of mud and taking the lives of both driver and fireman. Unfortunately the train that had been signalled, an Edge Hill-Leeds goods hauled by 'Special DXs' 1355 and 1890, ran into the wreckage, while a similar engine, No. 1807 on a Leeds to Burton beer empties, also ran into the wreckage, miraculously without causing any further casualties. On the same spot, on 16th November, 1895, Great Northern Railway No. 591, a 2-4-0 on a Wakefield to Halifax express, similarly held, took signals for a Newcastle-Liverpool express

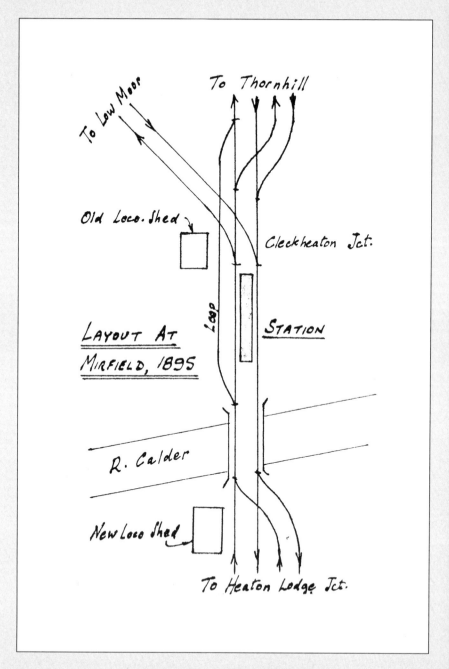

Diagram of track layout at Mirfield in 1895 where only two lines crossed the Calder until 1932 when it was widened by the LMS.

G.H. Brown

and was in sidelong collision with Edge Hill 'Precedent' No. 890 *Sir Hardman Earle*. On both occasions the breakdown gang cleared the wreckage under Goulding's supervision, in the former case without accepting relief for nearly 36 hours.

Goulding was also present nearby, a year or two later, for a bridge testing ceremony on the Leeds New Line pending the opening of that portion between Heckmondwike Jn and Northorpe to goods traffic before the remainder of the line was brought into use in 1900. A gigantic 270 ft-span Warren bridge over the Calder at Battyford was subjected to testing by running a pair of 'Johnny Duggan' 'B' class 0-8-0 compounds coupled together with a Coal Engine at front and rear. This powerful combination started from Battyford like an enormous monster unleashed, accelerated to a high speed only to come to an abrupt halt on the bridge after exploding detonators indicated where brakes were to be applied. With variations this spectacular performance was repeated four times, much to the delight of spectators who looked on from a safe distance.

After 38 years in the higher ranks Goulding retired and was followed by a man whose leadership was electrifying - Thomas Cheetwood. Whatever had been done well was done even better and several engines under his care went seven years without once visiting Crewe for overhaul. No job was too big and no detail too small to escape his attention (engines waiting the return of new tyres, tubes, cylinders, etc., would be dumped at the back of the shed on a dead end siding known as Wapping - how this name was bestowed or what it significance was is unknown). Cheetwood radiated a spirit amongst his men hitherto unknown, but woe betide anyone attempting to pull the wool over his eyes.

Those summoned before him on disciplinary matters would enter his office to the command, 'cap off, hands out of pockets, and stand on the mat!' He would detect the errors of judgement, the weakness of character, his shrewd mind having the knack of probing the most unlikely and unsuspected inadequacies. Although having but one eye, he could walk through the shed and accurately tell upon which engines cleaners and bar boys would be hiding!

During the railway strike in 1919 a patchy service was kept running by using staff and volunteers. Cheetwood drove No. 618, a 19 in. 0-6-0 on the first train to use the New Line to Leeds. The journey was without incident save for the number of passengers. Beyond Cleckheaton the line curves round into Gomersal tunnel on a 1 in 77 gradient with a curve at each end, and always attended by dampness caused by the constant presence of water. Gomersal tunnel had the reputation of being the second worst tunnel on the LNWR, only exceeded in this respect by the single line-tunnel leaving Liverpool (Lime Street). No sooner had the train entered than No. 618 slipped to a standstill, for some spiteful person had given the rails a liberal coating of wagon grease in anticipation of such a journey. The train had to be divided before passengers saw the light of day some two hours later, the engine returning for the hindmost portion later; as to the plight of the passengers, their feelings can best be left to the imagination.

Cheetwood's departure at the close of 1919 was a matter of general regret. He was at Wigan only a short time before moving to Longsight for a higher position.

The New Line at Heckmondwike under construction *c.* 1898 at a point that became Heckmondwike Goods. *Author's Collection*

Gomersal tunnel at the Cleckheaton end during construction. *Author's Collection*

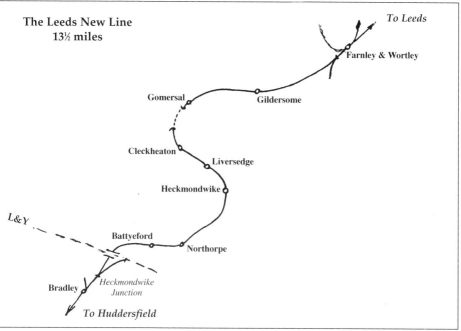

The Leeds New Line
13½ miles

To Leeds

Farnley & Wortley

Gomersal
Gildersome

Cleckheaton
Liversedge

Heckmondwike

L&Y

Battyeford
Northorpe

Bradley   *Heckmondwike*
            Junction

To Huddersfield

Diagram of Leeds New Line, opened in 1900.   *G.H. Brown*

The 270 ft-span Warren Bridge at Battyefore on 10th June, 1960.   *Author*

The shed now had three foremen in quick succession. From 1923 it was in the charge of W.G. Ward who, until retirement in April 1933, served for 46 years beginning with an apprenticeship at Rugby and then successive positions at Northampton, Walsall and Aston. The next incumbent reflected the changes brought about in the Central Division in the LMS. A Lancashire & Yorkshire Railway (L&Y) man, Stanley Muff, had charge when half the shed's allocation of engines consisted of ex-L&Y classes. The LNWR 5 ft 6 in. 2-4-2T, LNWR 5 ft 0-6-2 tank, Special tanks, Coal Engines and 'Cauliflowers' (18 in. goods 0-6-0) had given way to L&Y 0-6-0 saddle tanks, 2-4-2 radial tanks and 'A' class 0-6-0s, all of which were good and capable engines although those that used them preferred LNWR types. The acid test was whether the newcomers kept time.

During the period of public ownership there were five shedmasters. A recent one, Norman Howcroft, a man born and bred on the North Eastern Railway, had charge at a time when the consequences of the Scheme for the Reshaping of the Railways and the uncertain condition of steam locomotives was most evident. It could be said truly that he was a great 'doer' though unobtrusive by nature, and his encyclopaedic knowledge of locomotive engineering and enthusiasm were combined with an enlightened outlook of consideration and courtesy to both subordinates and visitors to the shed. Howcroft was the son of a late North Eastern Railway driver who was involved in a head-on collision just outside Hull Paragon station on 18th January, 1901 when arriving with the 3.35 pm from Leeds. He received serious injuries and upon being cut free discovered his railway timepiece, protected by a heavy brass hinged case, was still working. Norman Howcroft carried this with him into retirement, even though it bore a heavy gouge caused by the worm of the reversing gear.

Norman Howcroft, shedmaster at Hillhouse 1961-1965, formerly of Dairycoates, Alnmouth and Northallerton.   *Author's Collection*

Chapter Two

Some Outstanding Drivers

It has always been a popular practice for locomotives to bear the names of celebrities. George Sayles, a breezy character reversed this habit by christening one of his sons after his engine of the day, *John Rennie* a Webb 2-4-0 'Precursor' used in the early 1890s on the 4.45 am Huddersfield to Manchester slow train. One is tempted to speculate what he would have called his son, had he been employed by the Great Western as driver of engine No. 5069! Following the conversion of the 'Precursors' to 5 ft 6 in. 2-4-2Ts, a 6 ft 'Jumbo' took over the duty which was extended to work to Liverpool (Lime Street) returning from there at 12.12 pm on a slow train to Manchester South Jn running via Ditton Jn, Arpley and Broadheath. Following this the engine ran light to Stockport Edgeley to take out the 3.35 pm Bradford express. This, instead of using the normal route via Stalybridge, ran via Ashton Moss and passed Oldham, Ashton-under-Lyne & Guide Bridge (OA&GB) Jn only a few minutes after an express from Manchester Exchange to Leeds, before calling at Oldham Glodwick Road where it made its only intermediate stop. Despite the longer and vastly harder road, the train reached Huddersfield immediately behind the express. [See *Appendix One* for fuller details of engines mentioned in this chapter.]

In 1913 Sayles achieved fame on this turn using No. 1021, a superheated 4-6-2 tank, although the load seldom exceeded three bogies, he nevertheless used only 26 lb. of coal per mile, something others found hard to equal. This engine, and No. 2670, which worked to Stockport on another duty over the OA&GB line through Oldham to Rochdale, was placed in the same link as the Webb 5 ft 6 in. 2-4-2 tanks. If one of the larger engines was not available one of the latter would deputise. In 1921 a Whale 'Precursor' No. 1312 *Ionic* was assigned this duty, but its reign was short as three weeks later it moved to Farnley Jn Shed being succeeded by an 18 in. 0-6-0 goods engine No. 190 and then by No. 1418 *Cheshire,* the first 'Experiment' the shed was to have.

Sayles was once given a week's suspension by Goulding, for omitting to make a conditional stop at Saddleworth with a pick-up goods during the small hours. A stop which was rare indeed. Some time later he involuntarily levelled the score. It happened like this. One evening after finishing work he caught sight of some cleaners playing cricket at the back of the Fox and Grapes in Northgate and joined in. When it was his turn to bat, who should emerge from the back door of the pub but the foreman unsteady of foot, who with some difficulty made his way in the direction of a curiosity consisting simply of three large pieces of stone, one for the back and two set at right angles for the front. Once inside only the head of the occupant was visible. It was at such a moment that Sayles hit a Yorker which must surely have been a 'six' had it not made sharp contact with the foreman's head. When seen the following day Mr Goulding appeared none the worse for his unexpected loss of consciousness!

To ask who was the finest driver at Hillhouse one would receive one answer - 'Waggy' Metcalf. Billy Metcalf was born out of wedlock on 5th March, 1881. His

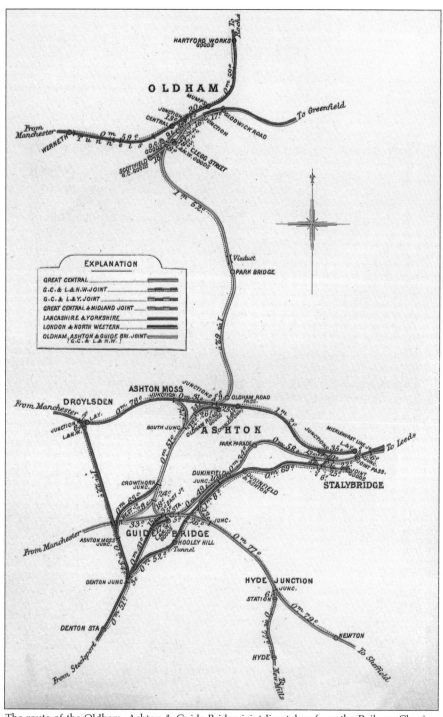

The route of the Oldham, Ashton & Guide Bridge joint line taken from the Railway Clearing House Junction Diagram book of 1912.

A rare line picture of a lined-out Coal Engine No. 2226 with George Sayles on the engine. This view was taken in 1904 when Hillhouse wagon repair shop was still extant, shown in the background.   *Ada Sayles*

A Webb 'Special DX' stands at Dewsbury in 1910 on a Leeds-Huddersfield train in the charge of driver 'Waggy' Metcalf.   *Author's Collection*

father was a driver named Fred Rushworth and his mother a doctor's servant girl. He was placed in a basket and left on the doorstep of Mrs Wagstaff. She could not face a new child being taken to an orphanage and brought him up as her own son - her own children all having grown up including Harold Wagstaff, the Rugby League prince of centres. The relationship was outstanding and later when Waggy started work, it was at Hillhouse Shed as cleaner. He was a good fireman at a young age and was sent to be interviewed at Crewe by F.W. Webb, 'Waggy' having been singled out with others of great promise to be transferred to Crewe, to learn all the roads with the prospect of becoming tomorrow's top link drivers. Sadly 'Waggy' related to Webb his strange position and Webb accepted that his first duty lay to his mother. Billy Metcalf became a driver at Hillhouse and worked in the 5 ft 6 in. tank link until taking retirement on 4th March, 1947. Then surprisingly a new chapter opened in his life and he worked in a woollen mill until 1952. He died in 1976.

A very famous driver once at Hillhouse was George Hinchliffe - the man described by Ahrons working No. 1 *Saracen* between Leeds and York. After this he had No. 1220 *Belted Willy* which later came to Hillhouse. A very tall bearded man with an infectious enthusiasm for his job,* and held in high esteem by his superiors, no locomotive inspector ever came aboard Hinchliffe's engine without first being invited. After the York turn was abolished at the end of 1905 he moved back to Farnley Jn Shed, by which time he must have been fast approaching the end of his time - one could not call it retirement as we know it today. Indeed the LNWR conduct sheet which recorded all the events during a person's working life very often concluded with the term 'retired - old age', sometimes when a driver was nearly seventy.

In contrast to Sayles, Harry Eastwood was quietly spoken and unassuming. His first footplate job was firing for Joe Warburton during the mid-1880s on No. 1977, an old Crewe Goods 2-4-0. Several of these were used as bank engines between Heaton Lodge and Marsden after displacement from passenger work by the new Webb 4 ft 6 in. 2-4-2 tanks. He related, 'not that they were much good, as the boiler was small and the firebox no bigger than a chestnut roaster', adding, 'sometimes when banking it got left behind by the train it was supposed to be pushing'. Once with Eastwood, Warburton stalled in Huddersfield tunnel and ordered his fireman to walk on the running plate, stand on the buffer plank and drop sand on the rails from a bucket, to which he received a most uncharacteristic reply: 'If you think I'm going to do that, then you've another think coming - you can lumpit!'

The best of these engines was reputed to No. 1950, George Mossley's old engine. During its lifetime the diameter of its cylinders had been bored out, and with a couple of piston rings wedged in the chimney, a 'jemmy' across the top of the blast pipe and the safety valves weighted down, it could perform amazing work out of all proportion to its size. All of these refinements were entirely taboo, but a blind eye was turned to the lifelong habits of drivers. Interestingly one never heard of any mishaps arising from their use. For many years there used to exist, along the wall facing No. 1 road, a line of boxes where such items were stored by drivers when not in use.

---

* Hinchliffe was working at Copley Hill LNWR shed in 1860 and compiled a list of engines stationed there in that year.

The term Bank engine was often used on the LNWR and indicated the engine would be diagrammed to be placed ahead of the train engine, e.g. Heaton Lodge to Diggle where it came off. It also shunted, did trip work and sometimes banked trains from the rear but was always referred to as a Bank engine.

The 'DX Goods' 0-6-0s, like the 'Crewe Goods' were used on all kinds of traffic, passenger and goods, and having a useful turn of speed it was not uncommon for one to be used on express work. On the other hand they were known to take 30 loaded coal wagons up to Marsden, before coming back with twice as many empties. If one was a feat of haulage, the other was of enginemanship of great skill and required a good understanding with the guard. Stopping such a train on a 1 in 96 gradient in a damp tunnel on the tender hand brake, reversing screw and guard's brake required nerves of iron, but this was an everyday occurrence, and those who did it thought little about it.

Just after 2-2-2-2 No. 20 *John Hick* was built in 1894, it was sent to Hillhouse on a week's trial on Leeds to Manchester stopping trains with George Mossley as driver and Eastwood as fireman, both of whom regarded it as unsuitable for the banks and the frequent stops it had to make, as when starting its driving wheels revolved in opposite directions. Nevertheless it had a very good boiler and there was never any problem with maintaining steam. The Webb compound passenger engines were rare on the Yorkshire lines. In 1890 Longsight worked a diagram that included a round trip between Manchester and Leeds with one of the first three 'Teutonics'. On 21st January, 1892 as No. 1302 *Pacific* was going very fast down the bank through Blakestones cutting the right-hand leading driving wheel broke loose and an astonished crew saw it running alongside them, before making an emergency stop at Slaithwaite without further mishap or casualties being caused. The engine was replaced and put on Hillhouse Shed before being sent to Crewe some days later. On the question of Webb compound engines, Eastwood was quite emphatic - they were 'fairish engines'. He never attempted to pour scorn on them. The only critical comment was of the 'Bill Bailey's' but not of their operation or haulage ability, but of their propensity for breaking down they were well named, he said. On the other hand there have been more renowned classes of engine with this same feature, but attracting none of the odium which it became fashionable to bestow on Webb engines.

Before he drove regularly, Eastwood sometimes worked excursions in the extra link with a 'Special DX' or an 18 in. Goods 0-6-0 to Bridlington and Scarborough and at certain times to Newcastle. One occasion he remembered was on the occasion of Longwood Thump, a local feast day when he set out for Whitby with a mill trip. At Malton a North Eastern inspector curtly informed him 'you can't take that up yonder'. 'That' was an almost new 18 in. Goods No. 879 and not unnaturally Eastwood felt rebuffed. It appeared the NER had some doubts about its ability to cope with the gradients, although Eastwood had none at all. Unfortunately he was never given the chance to prove it. After putting No. 879 on Malton Shed and damping down the fire, he and his mate got aboard the train, which had been split into three portions each of six 6-wheelers, being taken forward by a 'BTP' 0-4-4 tank on each. Returning to Malton on the first return portion and getting the engine ready to depart in the small hours of the

A 'Crewe Goods' 2-4-0, used as a bank engine, seen coming down from Bradley Wood Jn with Bradley tunnel in the background. It is passing beneath the Lower Cinderfield Dyke which is carried over the railway by a cast-iron aqueduct.   *Ian Fraser*

An '18 in. Goods' 0-6-0 No. 577 is being turned in August 1905. James Goulding, locomotive foreman, is seen standing next to the engine with driver Steve Denton in the cab.
                                                                                    Revd R.G. Johnson

next day, he ran non-stop through York to Leeds due to the absence of other traffic, something he had never done before.

On a Saturday night, a few years earlier, when firing on the Hull job, the return departure was set back by the NER for one hour in order to clear its own specials from Hull Fair. Eastwood had a clear run to Broomfleet where they were placed on the slow line, in itself not unusual, but at Staddlethorpe, the road was set for Doncaster and the signal box switched out. Prolonged whistling produced no response and Eastwood was ultimately sent to seek out the station master who lived some distance from the line and was greatly displeased with having his slumbers broken for a 'Wessie' train. The driver on this occasion, a rare character called Steve Denton, was 'three sheets to the wind' - he always claimed he could drive by instinct and that night proved it. Denton was one of a small group of drivers who appeared to live for all the ale they could drink - it was a common practice for him to run from Hillhouse to Hull overnight, then go to the pubs, where he accommodated the ladies with his charm and hospitality, then book on at Dairycoates in the evening and work back home without having any sleep at all! Steve Denton died on 15th November, 1912 aged 53.

Eastwood is personally remembered for his association with Ben Garner for whom he fired on 743 occasions between 1896 and 1917, but otherwise driving as a passed fireman.

Hillhouse Shed lost several men by emigration. In September 1898 four men departed for India: Tom Eccleston, Jim Thorrocks, Richard Sutcliffe and Tom Whiteley. Eccleston returned some years later minus an arm, lost in an accident, was reinstated and finished his time as night foreman. Thorrocks was an infectious character with great enthusiasm for his job. He always carried the Bible in his double trip basket, though this appeared needless as he knew most of it by heart. With such a man it sometimes was a temptation for others to tease, in the hope of being rewarded by some slip of the tongue. The nearest he came to this was at Mold Jn Shed on a bitter freezing night - as his fireman was standing on the tender tank taking water, the water pouch slipped from beneath his foot and fell, drenching Thorrocks to the skin, to which he exhorted, 'Oh God, to whom vengeance belongeth, show thy hand!'* He drove home that night in borrowed nightshirt and greatcoat.

No one ever got the better of Thorrocks in an argument; at times a score of 'top people' had eaten humble pie. He had a memorable clash with the Manchester district superintendent, Henry Linaker, who narrowly missed being struck by a large lump of coal which fell from his tender as he entered Stalybridge from Stockport. This was of a size common enough in steam days, being moved by both outstretched arms. The whistle was sounded but to no effect. Linaker had not recovered from the shock of a near miss when Thorrocks, true to style, comforted him with, 'Take ye heed, watch and pray, for ye know not when the time is!'†

One of the few Hillhouse men bestowed with nicknames was Joe Warburton, a somewhat eccentric figure, having the distinction of being known as 'Lightning' owing to his marked reluctance to run. This was said to be a product of receiving severe head injuries in an accident which legend said

---

* St Mark 13. 33.

† Psalm 96. 1.

Tom Eccleston, a Hillhouse driver who was one of four who went to work on the Indian Railways in 1898. He is seen here on return to the shed, minus his left forearm. He finished as Hillhouse night foreman.

Russell Wattam

necessitated the insertion of a silver plate to his skull. When his sanity was questioned, as it sometimes was, he had been known to produce an official looking printed certificate pronouncing that the bearer was 'alright', which, he claimed was more than some others had to show! It was once claimed that his end would come either through being run into by another train from behind or else being struck by lightning!

One Sunday before the Standedge double-line tunnel had been started he and Fred Johnson had been working a Standedge ballast train, and were about to return to shed when Warburton succeeded in putting the tender off the rails through some trap points.

By this time they had been working for more than 12 hours and Johnson, only too well aware of his driver's reputation, put some Epsom Salts into his tea bottle in an attempt to expedite matters. No doubt they made good time on the way back to Hillhouse.

The discovery of a body on rough land adjoining the shed in 1870 prompted much murmuring in the neighbourhood. The body was unidentified and the cause of death unknown. The result was rumour and reports of ghostly goings on. A few weeks later as a group of cleaners were sent out 'knocking-up' they walked along Whitestone Road when a figure clad in black and white stripes appeared suddenly from a doorway. The three youths struck out furiously and repeatedly, and as one said later 'we flayed the ghost of Hillhouse'. The episode closed when the three youths ended up in court charged with assault. A doctor had left his nearby home to attend a patient; leaving a sudden gust of wind caught his dressing gown and gave him the spectral quality of the Hillhouse ghost. Mr E. Winby, locomotive foreman, spoke on behalf of the three cleaners in court. Mr Winby during his tenure at Hillhouse also had responsibility for locomotives used during the making of Blackmoorfoot Reservoir, and on one occasion found a locomotive had been lit up without the boiler first being filled.

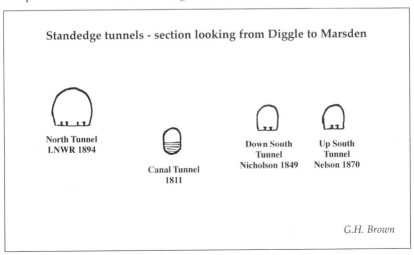

Standedge tunnels - section looking from Diggle to Marsden

North Tunnel
LNWR 1894

Canal Tunnel
1811

Down South Tunnel
Nicholson 1849

Up South Tunnel
Nelson 1870

G.H. Brown

Stalybridge station looking west, the two L&YR bays are to the right. The line to Manchester Victoria diverges from the M&SL Guide Bridge lines in the centre and the widened LNWR lines via Hooley Hill and Stalybridge goods and coal yard are on the left.   *Author*

Standedge tunnel looking west from the Marsden end on 11th April, 1949. To the left we see Tunnel End siding, the Nelson (1871) and Nicholson (1849) tunnels. Canal Reservoir overflow double line (1894) tunnel is on the right and out of view to the right and at a lower level is the Huddersfield Canal tunnel.   *Author*

Chapter Three

In his Habit as he Lived

At a time when relations between the company and its workforce left something to be desired, the Amalgamated Society of Railway Servants' secretary at Hillhouse Shed was Tom Topping, a vibrant character who could speak to anyone regardless of their position.

Two concessions granted to footplate crews during Topping's time include the increased time allowed for preparing engines, which on 17th May, 1907 was increased from 30 to 45 minutes in the case of small engines, while for big engines the period was improved from 45 minutes to an hour. This came about when preparation time for a Coal Engine compared with that of a 'B' class 0-8-0 and 19 in. 4-6-0 Goods were quite dissimilar. In 1912 all crews began to receive one week's paid holiday annually, a concession more than 37 years ahead of general adoption. For the engineman it meant travel for him and his wife and children to some resort at quarter fare. Ben Garner on his first such holiday in 1913 travelled to Omeath,* about as far as he could go on LNWR metals.

For all the hardship of long hours, bad weather and surrounded by countless hidden dangers which sometimes ended in instant death, life on the footplate had its compensations for the driver was the uncrowned King of working men. Once, when advising an impulsive fireman who had been disciplined, Topping retorted, 'there's no wit like bought wit!' On another occasion he observed, 'A man is not rich by what he owns, but more by what he can do without, with dignity'.†

Topping, a lifelong atheist, was the first man from the shed elected to Huddersfield Town Council and served from 1911 to 1921, also serving as a Justice of the Peace from 1913. The performance of public duties involved considerable sacrifice and to compensate him, and later a few others similarly engaged, the Huddersfield Labour Party set up a special fund for that purpose. The pioneer in social change was a lone figure in those early days.

In 1897 Topping had charge of newly built 5 ft 6 in. 2-4-2 tank No. 1367 which was double-manned with Ben Garner. On his first trip out, on the 5.02 pm Stockport to Leeds he knocked out the left-hand eccentric strap and also broke a buffer! The engine returned home on the 9.30 pm 'all stations' Leeds New to Huddersfield, and shortly afterwards both drivers were recipients of publicity for their exploits. The *Huddersfield Examiner* carried a letter headed 'Enginemen as ticket collectors':

> I was a passenger on Saturday night last . . . and after much endurance in both Leeds station and also by other means into which I shall not enter in this letter, at last reached Bradley, where tickets were to be collected, but, strange to say, the ticket collectors were off duty, and after some delay the fireman and driver jumped off the engine, one of these appeared at the door of the compartment in which I was seated and collected tickets. This duty over, the engine was remounted, and we set off at reckless speed, and with much oscillation, finally reached Huddersfield in safety about half an hour late.

* Omeath, on the Dundalk, Newry & Greenore Railway was an LNWR outpost in Co. Louth opened on 1st May, 1873 as a 13 mile 5 ft 3 in. gauge extension of the Holyhead-Greenore steamship service and along the shores of Carlingford Lough.
† Thycudeses

On the other hand, on 17th January, 1898, as Garner, working the same train, ran into Batley he overshot on a greasy rail and the end of his train ended up nine feet beyond the platform ramp. A young man travelling in the last compartment engaged in conversation with a lady, bade her good night, and with his back to the open door got out and fell on to the lineside causing himself serious injury. The matter was taken to Leeds Assizes before Mr Justice Darling and a jury. The LNWR was represented by Tindall Atkinson, QC. Five examples of case law were cited in favour of the defendants' denial of negligence and coupled with Atkinson's claim: 'If passengers were not expected to exercise such ordinary care in alighting it would be necessary for railway companies to strap them in!' The learned Judge withdrew the case from the jury and gave judgement in favour of the company. An appeal was lodged and the Court of Appeal found that the Judge should have left the decision to the jury and ordered a new trial, where judgement was reversed and the plaintiff was awarded £150 damages, but ordered to pay costs!

Topping had a memorable encounter with F.W. Webb after the saloon of the latter had been unexpectedly added to the back of his train at Stalybridge. The delay caused Topping to run fast. When the train emerged from Standedge tunnel and round the reverse curves into Marsden the King of Crewe's tail really wagged, and on reaching Huddersfield Webb stormed up to the engine waving his umbrella and exclaimed, 'You have just come from Stalybridge in 21 minutes . . .' But before he had chance to finish, Topping retorted, 'We did it in 19½ last night!' On his death in 1933, instead of a normal Christian burial, a spokesman for the Labour Party read an address at his graveside. The newspaper obituary with photograph of him standing on the footplate of a 5 ft 6 in. 2-4-2 tank bore the inscription - 'In his habit as he lived', a truly great and fascinating man.

Tom Topping, councillor 1911-1921 and magistrate from 1923 had the rare attribute of being able to speak to anyone and command attention.   *Author's Collection*

Chapter Four

Men on the Shed

It used to be an eight hour task to clean an engine that by modern standards would be immaculate to start with. Nevertheless it required determination in mid-winter when icicles hung from the sanders and snow covered the buffers. Often a proficient cleaner found that his ambition to fire lay a long way ahead; when he did reach the footplate it would be that of a shunting engine, progressing to that of a pick-up goods and always learning - to fill the sandbox, to keep the ashpan clean, not to choke the fire, to fill the tender tank, look out for signals, learn the road, while his ear would become trained to detect the slightest variation from normal. There were those who never reached the footplate by reason of sight or hearing, but who did much of the shed routine work, for example the knocker-up (who raised the footplate crews from their slumbers), often one of the first tasks for a new cleaner, washer-out, steamraiser, lamp man and coaler.

When an engine was in need of repair, it would be seen first by an examining fitter. George Pierce occupied this position for many years, and armed with the tools of his job, a duck lamp and hammer, would ascertain what would be needed to put matters right. It was a skilful occupation. A further duty included that of carrying out the statutory Board of Trade examination on privately-owned locomotives in the Huddersfield area. Following a wash-out the fire would be lit by Frank Knight, the steamraiser. Armed with a long-handled fire shovel weighing 47 pounds, Knight would board an engine in steam and from its firebox draw out a shovelful of coal, then aided by a duck board, place the shovel on his shoulder and jump over to an adjacent engine about to be lit up, a feat of great ability better watched than described and performed with all the precision of a drill movement. If the need was desperate steam could be raised in an hour to a sufficient level that would allow the engine to just move under its own power. If for any reason steam could not be raised a short cut sometimes practised would be for the engine to be given a 'bucket of steam': a bucket of water thrown on the fire. This was totally unauthorised for if the firebox door was not closed smartly by a second man, the thrower ran the risk of being scalded. It was practised only in certain circumstances, the fire having a depth of six inches and being red all over. The water caused an explosion whose force was directed through the flues removing any substance there, for example if an engine out of service for some time was lit up and caused the boiler to 'sweat'. It was always a matter of curiosity when visiting an engine shed, say late on a Sunday afternoon, to find in one part of the shed huge particles of soot, almost like cobwebs, and smoke hanging in the air - the result of someone having practised what has been described.

The water supply at Hillhouse came from the company's Slaithwaite canal reservoir fed into a 5 in. diameter pipe laid alongside the line between Slaithwaite and Heaton Lodge. When the water supply fell below the level of the line the supply ceased and locomotives were sent to Marsden to fill up. Although Slaithwaite reservoir was enlarged in 1864, the supply remained poor, especially

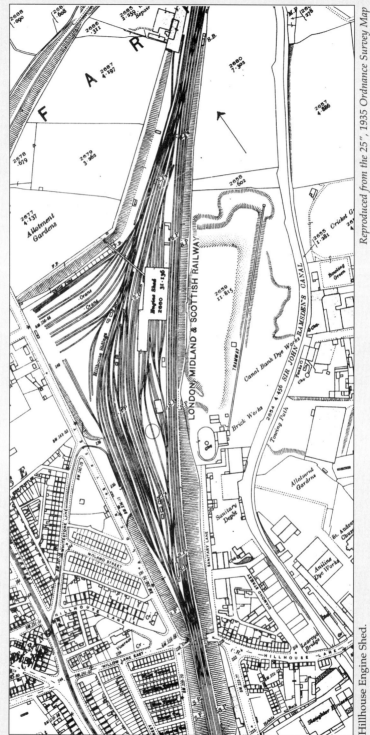

Reproduced from the 25", 1935 Ordnance Survey Map

Hillhouse Engine Shed.

during dry weather. On 19th July, 1871 a connecting pipe was laid from Summit Pool at Marsden to Slaithwaite after which the supply greatly improved.

Until 1930 low grade coal was the rule rather than the exception, produced at either Critchley, West End or Howley Park pits all of which were on the lineside to the west of Morley tunnel. Despite its low quality it was clean to use and did not easily clinker. Coal from other sources arrived during coal strikes, one consignment of very small Belgian coal arrived, and with it came of load of crickets that plagued the shed for months afterwards! If the fireman used the pricker often he had no trouble maintaining steam. In 1921, and again in 1948, some American coal arrived of good size and high quality, but difficult to light up. If the fire were kept thin some fierce heat would be produced.

Earlier, coal money would be paid to certain drivers, some of whom could earn sixpence a day. Others managed 13s. 8d. per quarter - that is to say 13s. for the driver and the odd coppers for the fireman if he were lucky. There were few regrets when the practice was abolished, although it did encourage economy. At every place where a stop was made, the lineside would be scanned for any coal that had fallen from someone else's tender - in fact anything that would burn did, and several yards of fencing to say nothing of the odd old sleeper, were known to have vanished in this way. It was by no means uncommon for some noted 'economist' to arrive at work with a couple of cauliflowers under his arms, or a couple of loaves as a goodwill gift to the coaler, who would return the compliment by loading the tender with more coal than was booked.

The coaling stage was worked by three men, one for each shift, employed on piece work and paid 4d. per ton for coal taken from drop-sided wagons, or 6d. per ton otherwise. It was quite usual for a man to move 24 to 28 tons during the course of a single shift and look after his own spillage.

The rule book was regarded by different persons in different ways, many having their own interpretation of particular rules, but a breach could result in the culprit receiving either a caution, reprimand or suspension. For anyone suspended it was nothing short of disaster and his family knew only too well what 'common sense' days were. Over-running a signal was always punished by suspension, it was not unusual for a driver in his fifties or sixties, after an unblemished career, to be in breach of the rule book and anyone of that group who managed to steer clear were indeed few and fortunate. Failing with age was part of a pattern of life for many.

One of the principal footplate necessities was food, carried in the wicker double-trip basket along with special notices, night-shirt, etc. A good appetite could be worked up on a long trip especially in raw weather. Many a hearty meal has been cooked on the shovel and eaten in a refuge loop pending the road being cleared, and eggs and bacon never tasted better than when done in this way. In winter a large onion would be roasted behind a gauge glass for five or six hours and eaten nice and juicy as a preventative for chest and throat ailments, while the tea bottle, filled with cold sweet tea, was a great stimulant for the weary.

The use of breakdown cranes in LNWR days was very much different from LMS times. Formerly it was quite common for a derailed engine to be dragged on the sleepers to the first set of points, regardless of the number of chairs broken and, moreover, quicker too.

The track at an engine shed usually received little attention from the Permanent Way Department. This view shows work taking place on the water tank and coal line.

Revd R.G. Johnson

Wheel turning - a pair of wheels from a Webb 5 ft 6 in. 2-4-2 tank, with James Goulding standing on the left. Alf Yougal, fitter, and George Pierce, the examining fitter, are on the right of the picture.

Revd R.G. Johnson

At the time of the Amalgamation with the L&Y pending the incorporation into the London Midland and Scottish Railway, F.W. Dingley was chief locomotive running superintendent before changing to be chief outdoor superintendent, and visited all sheds in a saloon hauled by locomotive 4-2-2 No. 3020 *Cornwall*.

A driver's tool box would contain the following:

Brake handle
Anti-vacuum clip
Claw spanner No. 17
No. 108 spanner ⅞ x ⅝ x ¼ (for lubricating steam brake cylinder).
No. 35 spanner ⅝ x ¾
No. 22 spanner ½ x ⅝
Trimming wire
Lamp wick
Duck lamp
Horse shoe nail - for cleaning burner in lamp
Firebox door spring
Oiler spring
Jemmy

The false lid would contain:

Rule book
Working timetables and appendix
Water tickets
Turn tickets - when using turntable of another railway, and if used twice in one week when on the same turn, a report would be asked for.
Wrong line tickets.

A group standing outside the shed office with Bill Riley, a senior driver holding lubricator, James Goulding, locomotive foreman, Alf Yougal, fitter, and Joe Noden, fitter are all seen.   *Revd R.G. Johnson*

Ben Garner on holiday at Douglas in 1904.   *Author's Collection*

The Garner family in 1905 taken near their home at Norman Park. *Back row, left to right*: Elsie, John and Hilda. *Front row, left to right*: Sarah Jane, Ben Garner, Francis Alice, Amy, Mrs Garner and Helena.   *Author's Collection*

Chapter Five

Ben Garner
and the Hull Job

Ben Garner (1860-1925) was born at Rowley Hill in February 1860 and after leaving school aged 12 worked in a pit until he was 14, when he became a cleaner at Hillhouse. He often went out in the small hours knocking-up. He was made a passed cleaner in 1876, then fireman, becoming a driver in 1887. At the time of his starting work the LNWR's Kirkburton branch had been in operation for only seven years and the second single-line Standedge tunnel opened three years earlier. The shed's allocation comprised Crewe Goods 2-4-0s, Ramsbottom 'DX' 0-6-0s with a miscellaneous collection of ageing 2-4-0 saddle tanks. Of these, the only engines having a steam brake were the tank engines, the brake on the others being simply a hand brake.

The Garner home was a back-to-back in Cowcliffe Hill to which the family moved in 1887. It was rented but never owned. A place where there was no debt, no hire purchase, no gambling and no drinking. Thrift was the watchword and prudence evident in everything. Most things were purchased at the Co-op, the Garner family being members of Hillhouse Co-op, which paid a dividend half-yearly, and the Huddersfield Co-op which paid quarterly. The importance of the Co-op 'divi' cannot be over-emphasised for there was no National Health or welfare benefits. Quarter stones of flour were purchased several times each week, and fresh bread baked on an iron range every alternative day, the range being black leaded every morning before the fire was lit. A plentiful supply of hot water was always available, providing the boiler was kept filled with a ladling can. As they grew up each member of the family had their own tasks to perform, choosing the joint for the Sunday dinner and cooking it being foremost, but also cleaning out the ashes from the previous day's fire, chopping the wood and fetching up from the cellar a bucket of coal and laying the fire, and afterwards making the beds. At the top of the house was the attic where the youngest members of the family slept. In a corner was a small stove and the window built in the sloping roof opened on a steel bar. In summer it was an airy place but in winter warm, snug and comfortable. On the first floor was the large bedroom used by the older girls, a smaller bedroom above the front door being used by Mr and Mrs Garner, while at the top of the stairs was a small landing accommodating a camp bed in which the only son slept - this may have had some bearing on the fact that on reaching 21 he married and left home!

Downstairs, behind the door was a hook upon which was hung a thick grey shawl plus a bobbin and a large key, (for the loo was through the passage and at the back, a tub lavatory changed every week by a gang of men who came with the 'marmalade' cart). Going to the loo in those days was not the most comfortable experience one would wish to make. The cellar head was a small room with a stone sink and cold water tap and a bucket beneath serving many purposes. The room was used for changing clothes, washing, etc., much as bathroom would do today. The cellar was divided into three: the coal cellar beneath the steps would contain about three tons of coal; the keeping cellar in the centre; and washing cellar by an open window with a 'set pot'. This was filled with water and fired by coke. Sheets and underwear would be boiled and Monday was the busiest with clothes being dried all round the house. A creel would be placed in front and above the fire, upon which ironed clothes were placed to air off.

Frances Martha Garner (1862-1937) was one of a small band of wise women found in every district. She was not only an engine driver's wife and mother to seven children, she combined the skills of a nurse, social worker and confidant to those seeking advice for a troubled mind.

She was present at confinements, terminal illnesses and laying out the dead, all done as a matter of neighbourly responsibility. The origins of public duty are often humble. Her life was one of hard work and self denial and saving for a rainy day.

From Ben Garner's starting work on the LNWR in 1874 the scene changed quickly. The LNWR 1877 Reddish-Leeds scheme envisaged doubling the entire Heaton Norris to Leeds route. Water troughs were installed in the twin-bore Standedge tunnels in 1878. Work commenced making Hillhouse yard in 1879, a task completed on 1st June, 1882.

The construction of Leeds viaduct began in May 1880 and opened as a new route on 1st June, 1882 but was preceded by the making of a new bridge at Canal Jn, Leeds opened on 14th November, 1881. Nearby Whitehall Road Goods depot, joint with the L&Y, opened on 1st November, 1880. The Denton Jn-Dukinfield Jn line was opened for goods on 2nd October, 1882 and for passengers on 1st November, 1882. Huddersfield viaduct was widened to five lines throughout its length between February 1882 and November 1883.

At Paddock the deep rock cutting was widened to accommodate four tracks starting in February 1881 while work began on making Huddersfield's second tunnel in 1883 and the enlargement of Huddersfield station began on 10th March, 1883. Meanwhile the section between Hillhouse and Heaton Lodge was widened in April 1884, including a new steel span over the Colne at Bradley and a new station with four platforms at Bradley.

On the route to Leeds widening of the L&Y main line between Heaton Lodge and Mirfield to the west side of the Calder viaduct, thence to Thornhill LNWR Jn, was completed in August 1884 but leaving double track through Mirfield.

Meanwhile widening of Longwood viaduct was completed in February 1884 and Manchester Exchange station was opened on 30th June, 1884. The Micklehurst line between Diggle and Stalybridge was opened on 1st December, 1885 for goods and on 1st July, 1886 for expresses, the portion at Stalybridge being initially worked single line when the original Huddersfield & Manchester Railway & Canal Co. Fairburn tubular girder spans were removed. At Huddersfield the enlarged station was completed on 5th June, 1886. A new bridge, the most westerly span of Huddersfield viaduct, replaced an inadequate masonry span on 10th March, 1883. Huddersfield goods yard and new goods warehouse was inaugurated on 18th July, 1885. Gledholt Sidings opened in June 1885, part of the space used dating from when spoil was dumped there during the making of the 1871 Nelson tunnel at Standedge.

At Longwood a new goods warehouse and yard was opened, while Golcar station dated from 1st March, 1889 and the widening between there and Slaithwaite was completed in September 1888. Linthwaite goods was commissioned on 14th August, 1889. The section between Slaithwaite and Marsden was widened in November 1891. At Dewsbury a major task was the reconstruction of the station in September 1889, the down platform being the major new work involved.

All these projects were carried out without interruption of traffic although excursions were curtailed, yet a regular interval service was introduced between Huddersfield and Leeds. At Standedge a new double-line tunnel was made between 1890 and 1894. Finally the Leeds New Line extending from Heckmondwike Jn to Farnley Jn was opened between Heckmondwike Jn and Northorpe for goods on 8th September, 1899 and the entire line was inaugurated on 9th July, 1900 for goods, passenger services starting on 1st October, 1900. Implementation saw the closure of Bankhouse Siding, Iredale's Siding, Scarwood Siding, Yorkshire Silica Works Siding, Morley Main Siding, Hardings Sidings, and Wards Sidings (to Engine Pit Colliery).

The first 24 years of Garner's LNWR service were to be one where change was the law of life. Everything evolved, nothing remained as it was, a period of growth unprecedented in British history. He was there at the start and saw it through this zenith of British railway development.

One of Ben Garner's most unusual experiences in the passenger link occurred with Webb 4 ft 6 in. 2-4-2 tank No. 691 on 24th November, 1898. Working a Leeds stopping train, he was pulled up for signals at Kirkburton Jn. When these cleared, he discovered on releasing the brake, that instead of creating a vacuum, the pipe became filled with steam, taking time to clear. So that at those places where the brake was needed it was used sparingly to avoid recurrence. When No. 691 was later examined it was discovered that the pipe leading to the whistle stand joint had become perforated below water level.

In 1900 Garner transferred to the coal link (on 5th February, 1900) and to the double trip link on 27th April, 1902. This was considered to be the top link and involved running to Liverpool, Bescot and Hull, out one night and return the next. On Saturdays the Bescot turn was rostered to haul the 6.35 pm Euston-Wolverhampton dining car express north of Birmingham (New Street) and allowed 26 minutes inclusive of a two minute stop at Dudley Port. On weekdays one engine worked this train throughout, but on Saturdays no extra time was allowed for the change of engines. On August Bank Holiday Saturday 1902, 18 in. Goods No. 569 is said to have reeled off the 13 miles in 20 minutes with a load of four bogie coaches and eleven 6-wheelers. One can assume a few liberties were taken because the smokebox door was white when they reached Wolverhampton. On another occasion a derailment blocked the north end of New Street station, so that when the train from Euston arrived Garner was required to hook on to the tail and take the train out via Proof House Jn and Aston. Unfortunately the weather was filthy and, as fate would have it, the tender roof sheet was missing and both men were soaked to the skin almost before their night's work had begun.

On the same turn on 2nd August, 1903 David Senior and Jos Megson were run into by a Midland train while standing at New Street. Both survived, although bearing visible evidence of their injuries. The journey to Birmingham could be a laborious business, but following improvements at Crewe between 1900 and 1906 the work became easier.

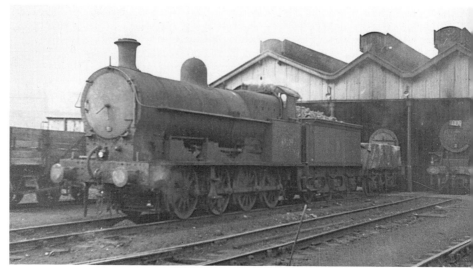

BR No. 49209, Ben Garner's most used 'D' class (as LNWR No. 734), used on 235 occasions prior to 1917. The engine is seen at Hillhouse Shed making a return visit in 1957 while shedded at Patricroft.   *Author*

LNWR No. 2277, an 0-8-2 tank used on Hillhouse coal chutes shunt and as Hillhouse bank engine from 1919. The term Bank engine in LNWR terminology is that of an assistant engine, usually added to the train being assisted at the the front and rarely banking from behind. This was Ben Garner's last engine as a two year period of ill health preceded his death in 1925.

P.F. Cooke

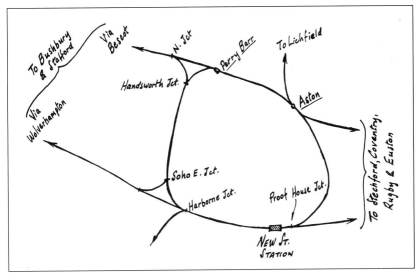

Diagram of Birmingham-Aston-Perry Bar and Soho Junction.   *G.H. Brown*

On 24th August, 1908 Garner became permanently employed on the Hull job, his opposite number outstationed at Dairycoates being Ben Tweedale who had 'Special DX' No. 1230, before receiving a new 19 in. 4-6-0 Goods No. 1399. The LNWR commenced running its own trains to Hull in 1893 and by 1900 engines from Farnley Jn, Longsight, Edge Hill, as well as Hillhouse, could be seen there regularly.

Garner's first engine on this work was No. 711, an 18 in. 0-6-0, later using No. 121, then No. 550 (all 18 in.) which lasted until 1912, although for short periods he had Nos. 8 and 2003 in 1909, both 19 in. 4-6-0s. From 1913 his regular engine was newly built 'G1' No. 734. His last trip to Hull on 1st August, 1914, when the LNWR goods workings were discontinued, was with a further 19 in. Goods, No. 81. Occasionally, when the Farnley Jn passenger engine outstationed at Hull had failed, Garner's engine would be substituted, necessitating his return home with a 'lame duck' and imposing some unlikely engines on the Hull-Liverpool passenger service.

Garner was a good man to work with and no one did more work on less steam, absolutely nothing was wasted and when his engine returned to shed the tender was invariably empty. It was said of him once: 'you'd think he owned the engine and had to buy the coal'. The only luxury he indulged in was holidays, and no family made better use of privilege tickets. Money was the yardstick by which everything was judged, saved from a life time of hard work and self denial for a rainy day that never came.

It was on the Hull job that he is mainly remembered, if only for beginning an enterprising sideline. Instead of returning home with an empty double-trip basket, his was filled with fruit, vegetables and fish obtained on the docks at very low prices. He also brought such things back for others who never travelled so far afield.   One is reminded of an incident one evening at Dairycoates Shed.   Curtis Ellsworth, the fireman of *Widgeon* the Farnley passenger engine there, sometimes went to the docks and on this occasion was asked by Garner to get him a *3d.* cod - that was Garner's limit - threepence. Doubtless due to his youth and inexperience he returned with a beautiful fish, wrapped in canvas and packed with ice for which he had paid *6d.* This was placed on the back of No. 121's tender and, on enquiry if the fish was suitable, was greeted with nodded approval and the placing on the running plate of a 3d. bit. 'I had to pay sixpence for that' said Ellsworth, but Garner feeling he was being taken in retorted 'threepence'.   To cut a long story short Ellsworth decreed, 'sixpence or else it will go in the firebox', whereupon cod, ice and canvas were given a quick dispatch. At this act of destruction Garner sadly murmured: 'Nay lad tha'a shouldn't done that, I'd rather given you half a crown'.   Perhaps it was an act of providence that the two never worked together!

When the Hull job was abolished Garner spent a whole week learning the road west of Huddersfield before acquiring No. 931, another 'G1' for double trips to Mold Jn, Crewe and Preston. Later on he worked on the London goods, the 9.20 pm from Hillhouse, and it was on the return working about 1924 that he was taken ill at Heaton Lodge and fell from the footplate. Recovery was slow and he was never the same after that and finished his time with No. 2277, an 0-8-2 tank Bank engine before another illness ended his life in June 1925.

A list of Garner's most used engines (and his firemen)* during 1896-1917 would comprise:

Engines

18 inch 0-6-0 Goods	No. 121	432 times	(LMS 8525/BR 58400)
18 inch 0-6-0 Goods	No. 903	425 times	(LMS 8456)
18 inch 0-6-0 Goods	No. 550	410 times	(LMS 8586)
'D' Class 0-8-0 Goods	No. 734	231 times	(LMS 9209)
18 inch 0-6-0 Goods	No. 914	235 times	(LMS 8587)
18 inch 0-6-0 Goods	No. 2325	184 times	(LMS 8412)
4 ft 6 inch 2-4-2 tank	No. 691	175 times	(LMS 6516)
18 inch 0-6-0 Goods	No. 625	153 times	(LMS 8368)
'G' Class 0-8-0	No. 1464	141 times	(LMS 9101)
18 inch 0-6-0 Goods	No. 879	136 times	(LMS 8332)
Coal Engine 0-6-0	No. 2387	142 times	(To Manchester & Milford Railway No. 8 4/04)
18 inch 0-6-0 Goods	No. 9	103 times	(LMS 8484)
'Special DX' 0-6-0	No. 1368	42 times	
19 inch 4-6-0 Goods	No. 81	40 times	(LMS 8794)

Firemen

F.H. Eastwood	743 turns	W. Hitchman	297 turns
C. Reid	350 turns	A.E. Turner	280 turns
Herbert Wadsworth	346 turns		

---

* Source Ben Garner's diaries 1896-1917.

Chapter Six

The News and 'Th'Owldam' Branch

One of the crack passenger turns during the late 1890s was performed by a 'Special DX' or 18 inch Goods 0-6-0, or, if one should be available, a 6 ft 'Jumbo' and involved working the 2.30 am Newspapers from Manchester Exchange to Leeds non-stop. For this 60 minutes was allowed for the 32 miles distance. From Stalybridge either the old route via Greenfield or the newer one via Micklehurst would be used as the gradients on the latter, although not as easy, were more consistent all the way to Diggle. After a three mile gallop through Standedge, the News would come down the Colne Valley as fast the engine would go, and if the board was 'off' at Springwood Jn would race through Huddersfield at over 60 mph about 35 minutes after leaving Manchester. Such a speed here is unheard of today, anything going at half that is considered to be moving. The line then falls all the way to Thornhill LNW Jn where the L&Y Wakefield line diverges. It then climbs through Dewsbury and steepens from Batley to Howley Park. The rest is easy. If the train should be favoured with a clear road it would reach Leeds in no more than 53 minutes, with a finishing sprint down from Morley that would make a Trans-Pennine diesel look pedestrian. After the New Line was opened in 1900 the train was routed that way to avoid the congested L&Y line at Mirfield, but the route was even more challenging.

It was George Sayles' privilege to work the first passenger train up the New Line. This occurred one Sunday before the official opening. A theatrical special from Liverpool which he took over at Huddersfield had arrived late due to permanent way work. An inspector travelling on the engine then informed him that 'there's to be no dillying about'. 'Y'ond', said Sayles some time later, 'had no need to concern himself', adding, 'I didn't 'arf make them Mary Annes sit up goin' down the bank from Gildersome'. The journey time of 22 minutes did not allow for such luxuries as slowing for the crossover at Farnley Jn or the reverse curves entering Leeds New. The inspector, however, left the footplate without speaking a word, the whiteness of his face expressing all that was needed.

The Oldham branch was a fearsome line to work, climbing away from Greenfield at 1 in 75, easing to 1 in 110 through Springhead tunnel which was invariably dripping wet and always filled with smoke. Leeds Shed worked most of the trains. Hillhouse had about three duties including one that left Greenfield in the small hours. It was on this particular train on a day in 1893, when there was a foot of snow on the ground, that George Mossley and Jos Atkinson stalled inside the tunnel with 'Special DX' No. 114. No matter how or what they did they could get no further and the atmosphere became so thick that both men left the footplate and lay on the ballast with a sponge cloth covering their faces. After several abortive attempts to restart, Mossley walked back the length of the train and on reaching the brake van discovered the guard fast asleep and the hand brake hard down, the train having run uphill for the best part of a mile in this manner.

There were few through trains to or from Yorkshire that ran over the OA&GB line, but after a mishap Mossley came over with the Mirfield butter train. The

Greenfield Jn with the Oldham branch on the right, climbing away at 1 in 75. Branch passenger trains often used the recessed platform with the water tank at the end.

Author

OA&GB rises 225 feet mainly at 1 in 70 between Ashton and Oldham and is no place to take a heavy train, but those who have no choice in the matter have to do the best they can. Mossley, regardless of load or gradient, had never been known to ask for assistance. He always maintained, 'if the engine will go I will manage'. If he had been told to go up Snowdon, I don't think he would have asked for an assistant engine! On this occasion, despite his undoubted gifts as an engineman he was not equal to the outsize job destiny had assigned him, stalling at Limehurst Pit and having to take the train up to Sheepwashers Lane in two portions.

But his troubles were not yet over, for as he neared Sett Siding (the top of the gradient of the line at Lees), a coupling broke and by Grotton he dare not brake in case the loose portion should come up at full speed behind him as he went down the bank. He shot out of Springhead tunnel on the top side of 50, and as the Greenfield outer home was 'on' a journey to the next world seemed imminent, yet strangely as he sped out of control past the signal, his eyes standing out like chapel hat pegs, it changed to 'off'. He roared through Greenfield Jn, pulling up some distance further up the line to Diggle without further mishap.

The foot of the incline has been the graveyard of several runaways. On 14th November, 1893 a 37-wagon coal train from Mosley to Oldham was reversed onto it, the engine then ran round but had not been recoupled when the guard released his brake, and like a great tidal wave the whole lot ran away, piling up against the station wall.

The reason why the LNWR did not carry much through traffic by this line was because they would have had to share receipts for it with the Manchester, Sheffield & Lincolnshire Railway (MS&L), which was joint owner. Coal traffic produced in the vicinity of the OA&GB line never quite matched expectations, much being taken by the Hollinwood and Limehurst branches of the Ashton Canal, owned by the MS&L.

Chapter Seven

The Birstal 'Coddy'

Although worked by Hillhouse men, the Birstal branch engine was supplied by Copley Hill Shed.* For many years a Webb 2-4-0 tank No. 2280 inhabited Birstal Shed, which was behind the platform. This single line structure, disused for more than 50 years, existed until 1960 when, together with the station, it was demolished, the water column remaining at the platform end.

A noted driver here in the 1870s and 1880s was Billy Bell, who had a son of the same name as fireman who did the boiler wash-out on a Sunday and lit up early next morning. He once saved the terminus from destruction when the adjoining mill caught fire in December 1888, and by sounding the engine whistle summoned the station staff to evacuate the premises. At the time Birstal had a family atmosphere. Bell's cousin John Woods was station master while two other of his cousins were employed as guard and head shunter respectively. Once after shunting, Bell backed down on the single coach standing in the platform, and after getting the 'right away' reached Carlinghow before noticing he had no train behind him! When invited to account for what had occurred he exonerated himself by exclaiming, 'You can pick your friends but you can't choose your relations'.

Originally most journeys ran from Dewsbury where the train used a short bay on the down platform, but latterly it terminated at Batley using a similarly positioned bay.

One Saturday night as the last train was pulling out, Bell was hailed by someone with a posh accent, 'Stop. I want to get on' but this had occurred before, and Bell, determined to administer a lesson on the benefits of punctuality shouted back, 'Thaa's too late, but you're first on t'platform for th'next'. The next, need it be said, was on the following Monday morning.

An interesting mishap occurred on 12th December, 1861 as the last train from Birstal was coming into Batley. The train was halted short of the main platform so that a van next to the engine could be placed on the transfer road. This was uncoupled and the engine ran it forward, meanwhile the guard and some porters commenced to push the two coaches into the platform. These were crowded, and just as they had begun to move they were run into by their engine whose driver Isaac Law was running back to haul them into the station. There was a near riot amongst the passengers. All the lights went out and then someone struck a match and lamp oil caught fire, but by luck failed to do any real damage.

The last driver to be outstationed at Birstal was Billy Underhill. The practice of having an engine there ended when the electric trams began taking their toll and services were slashed to but four trains a day. 'Undrill' was a dignified figure and a friend of James Goulding. During the 1911 strike Billy Underhill remained at work and returned home on one occasion to discover the front of his house had been whitewashed.

* Copley Hill Shed was replaced by Farnley Jn Shed in 1882.

The Birstal 'Coddy' passing Brookroyd Mills near Birstal about 1900. The mill still exists today and the trackbed has been landscaped.   *Author's Collection*

Batley looking east with a 'Chopper' tank running round the branch train. An 'Alfred the Great' class 4-4-0 compound is approaching from Leeds. The goods yard is on the left while the GNR line to Bradford Exchange and Leeds Central can be seen on the right.   *Author's Collection*

Driver William Underhill. He was the last regular driver of the Birstal 'Coddy'.

Author's Collection

View of Birstal terminus as a 'Chopper' leaves for Batley in the 1890s.   *Ian Fraser*

The approach line to Birstal Shed on 28th June, 1949. The water crane on the platform was still in use.   *Author*

The branch engine worked all the passenger duties, did most of the shunting but the principal goods duty was hauled by a Hillhouse 18 inch Goods, which left the terminus at around 5.00 pm destined for Liverpool. In its day it was quite a crack train. At one time the exit from the branch was controlled by a small signal alongside a much taller one, which usually remained 'off' for the 'Coddy' to run into the bay. One day instead of being allowed off the branch, the Liverpool goods was held while a procession of specials went past. Its driver Ambrose Leeming, expecting a long wait, picked up his billy can and before vanishing to a nearby hut, said to his fireman a young lad named Billy Willsdon, 'I want that signal before we move'. Twenty minutes later Leeming reappeared with his can filled with tea and to his astonishment saw his fireman about to manhandle the complete signal onto the footplate! This may have had some bearing on the fact that Willsdon acquired the nickname 'Strangler', by which he was afterwards more usually known. Leeming lost a leg in Hillhouse Yard not long after on a foggy night, and consequently finished his time as shed lamp man.

Willsdon, a giant of a man, was something of a weightlifter and was always in demand by fitters when the heavier parts were being removed from an engine under repair. He did this with ease and the gentleness of a lamb. One of his lesser achievements was to take on all comers at racing the width of the shed across eight lines of pits, with a fire bucket filled with sand in either hand. This spectacle came to a climax one day after someone 'tied' and the contest was restaged, not with sand, but with water and inevitable consequences.

An incident fixed in the memory of those present at the time began when a consignment of heifers was being unloaded in the goods yard. One of them took fright, broke loose and ran all over the yard before stampeding towards the shed, running down a pit and becoming trapped beneath an engine under repair. The engine had to be dragged out before the terrified beast could be extricated.

The terminus at Birstal on 9th April, 1960 with 'WD' 2-8-0 No. 90332 shunting in the distance. The station buildings had just been demolished revealing a length of track where the shed used to stand, on the right. *Author*

Enlargement of a photograph that is frequently described as the first train to Kirkburton. On the day in question the engine was decorated with flags and evergreens and heavy rain fell. This view is thought to have been taken on 31st May, 1868, the engine bringing empty coaching stock into Kirkburton goods yard prior to an excursion departing to Bangor at 5.00 am the next morning, 1st June, and making its return at 2.00 am on Sunday. The photograph is often credited as having been taken by G.T. Rhodes who was born in 1860, this would seem to be an error. Rhodes had by 1885 become a speaker on Railways, Scotland and bridges, etc. and this picture was probably used by him when addressing magic lantern show audiences in Sunday Schools and village halls. *Author's Collection*

A view of 4 ft 6 in. tank No. 825 about to be coaled. This engine was used on Kirkburton motor trains between April and September 1925. The class was displaced by Webb Coal Tanks. *Author*

Chapter Eight

Kirkburton Dick

The Birstal branch was the first LNWR Yorkshire branch to close to passengers in 1917 and the Kirkburton branch was to follow in 1930, being subject to intense bus competition from the mid-1920s. The bus service was provided by many operators offering a five minute frequency and a 5*d*. fare from Huddersfield. The Kirkburton train was known affectionately as 'Kirkburton Dick' a name that endures to this day, although the line closed completely in 1965. Between the ending of passenger services and the start of World War II, excursions and holiday trains operated.

The LNWR 4 ft 6 in. 2-4-2 tanks were used from 1884 and, from September 1916, maintained a motor service until replaced by 0-6-2 Coal Tanks in 1925, although these were displaced for a few months when three ex-Midland 0-4-4 tanks took over along with Midland motor coaches. Needless to say these were unpopular, although time was usually kept.

On 5th September, 1884 Tom Clough was driving 4 ft 6 in. tank No. 286 into Fenay Bridge, when by some mischance he was diverted into the goods yard, ploughing into two loaded gunpowder vans which were reduced to match wood, but fortunately did not explode.

The branch was never one of Harry Eastwood's regular haunts, although once after a failure he went up the line with No. 1148 *Boadicea*, a 5 ft 6 in. 2-4-0 'Precursor', which he described as a 'fairish engine'. She slithered so much on the final 1 in 66 into the terminus that passengers alighted from the train and walked past as it was moving!

Arthur Rozengrove, a coarse-grained inflammable character, once worked the branch goods on a wild day when the rails were covered in drizzle. Numerous attempts were made to restart from Kirkheaton on the 1 in 71. This caused delays to other traffic and on the return to shed he was instructed to report to the foreman. The rebuke from Goulding was the last straw and after suppressing his anger finally let flow a torrent of words which the foreman had rarely heard before, concluding with 'What th'aa wants for a driver is a chap aar't t'infirmaary - baat legs' - someone who wouldn't slip!

During the General Strike only one train ran on the branch, hauled by 18 in. 0-6-2 tank No. 189 and driven by a strike-breaking fitter named Longbottom, who forgot to take water before they left Huddersfield and by the time the terminus was reached the fire had to be thrown out as the boiler was almost dry. No. 189 remained at Kirkburton until the dispute was over. As for the unfortunate Longbottom, he was to work at the shed in a world of silence. As a strike breaker no one would talk to him.

The Webb Coal Tanks resumed passenger duties and No. 7700 worked the final train but, without any of the formalities that so marked closures in much later years. That portion of line between Kirkburton Jn and British Dyes Siding remained open until 25th February, 1971.

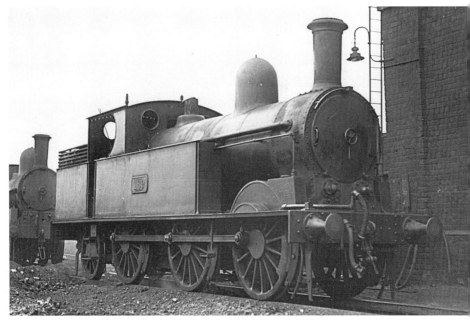

LNWR No. 189 hauled the only train to Kirkburton during the General Strike but ran out of water and remained at the terminus until the strike was over.   *P.F. Cooke*

Three Midland Railway 0-4-4 tanks were tried on the Kirkburton branch with No. 1277 arriving in November 1927. They were replaced by Webb Coal tanks within a year.   *Real Photographs*

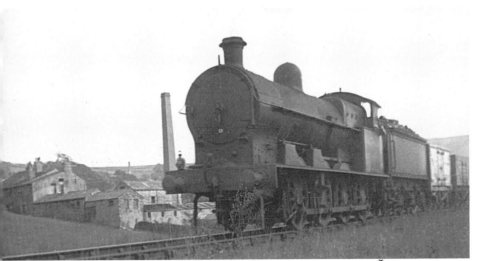

An unidentified LNWR 0-8-0 leaves Elliott's siding, on the Kirkburton branch, in 1933.
W.B. Stocks

Derailment at Elliott's siding when No. 9361 came off the line (which was linked to narrow gauge lines at a higher level) on 25th May, 1948. *Author's Collection*

Ex-Works No. 49323 is seen on the 4.05 am Edgeley-British Dyes siding as it passes Deighton on 6th August, 1960. Hillhouse men worked this train from Hillhouse sidings and driver Stanley Lake is at the regulator.   *Author*

The demolition train at Fenay Bridge & Lepton station on 30th July, 1966. From left to right: guard McQuillan, inspector Les Jardine, fireman Frank Stephenson and driver Harry Cole.   *Author*

Chapter Nine

The Crime Sheet and
Bradford Wool Traffic

The crime sheet was an historical document which commenced on one side with the date and place of appointment, rate of pay and particulars of promotion, reductions and injuries received. A driver may have been 'put back firing' or a fireman 'put back cleaning' either through shortage of work, or in rare cases as a disciplinary measure. More usually a driver would be reduced to a shunting link at his own request by reason of health. This side of the document concluded with a space for the termination of employment with the reasons for this being given. 'Retired - old age' was common in the late 1920s. The other side of the sheet bore the heading PUNISHMENTS (black ink) and GRATUITIES (red ink). Entries in red ink were almost unknown, while anyone who escaped some sort of endorsement belonged to a very small minority. It was almost too easy to be 'late off shed, causing delay to other trains', while 'failing to report for duty' signified the recipient had overslept, offences of a nature usually marked 'cautioned'.

A fitter who failed to detect a defect causing a late start or engine failure, a driver 'blowing off when entering Mirfield station dislodging dirt, soot, etc. and damaging passengers' clothing', failing to see that Rule No. 55 was promptly carried out, or exceeding the speed limit at Ring Road Bridge, Farnley Jn would invariably produce a reprimand, and the comments 'more serious notice to be taken if again at fault' were self explanatory. To pass a signal at danger would merit at least one day's suspension, and if it were on the main line, three or four days would be given. Yet dismissals were few and only for repeated serious offences. Only a few incidents come to mind in this respect, the persons involved having lead charmed lives beforehand.

The events are not without interest. The first concerns Fred Haigh who once, after dropping some vans off the Mirfield butter train at Broadheath, slipped off with his mate to a public house. They resumed their journey to Edge Hill, but both of them nodded off in the hot sun and eventually ran through the crossing gates at Latchford station taking a hay cart with them. This was before the Manchester Ship Canal deviation line was made.

Haigh's dismissal occurred on a day on which ironically he was perfectly sober. On Good Friday 21st April, 1905 after booking on, Haigh was asked to take Webb 4-6-0 compound No. 610 to Huddersfield to be turned, the engine, a 'Bill Bailey' too large to be turned on shed. When he arrived at the station three parcels vans blocked the turntable. These were drawn out onto Huddersfield viaduct and set back to the up main at Huddersfield station. The engine was then turned and had returned to where the three parcels vans had been left; unfortunately he set off on the wrong line and collided head-on with L&Y 2-4-2 tank No. 664 arriving from Bradford and caused the deaths of two persons. The company held its own inquiry the same day, and issued a statement informing the public that Haigh had been dismissed - before either inquest or Board of Trade inquiry. Tom Topping protested about the manner of the dismissal but his plea went unheard.

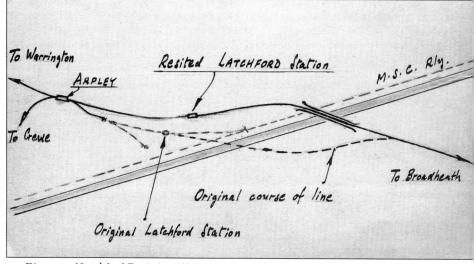

Diagram of Latchford Deviation 1894.   *G.H. Brown*

A Bradford Exchange to Bristol woolbuyers' special on Golcar brook viaduct about 1907. When the route was quadrupled the viaduct was separated from the original structure by about 10 feet.

Author's Collection

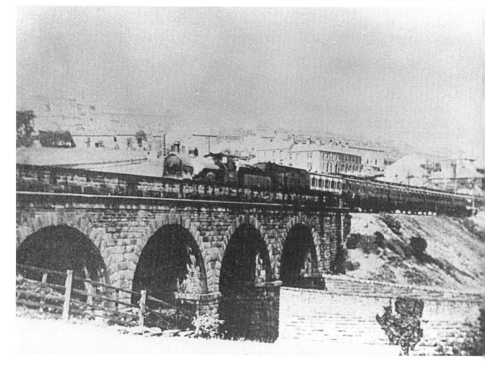

Just after motor trains had been introduced on the Kirkburton branch in 1916, Abe Roberts, a driver in the Kirkburton link, started an association with a lady passenger when the latter travelled to Huddersfield on the first train. Roberts would leave his controls and travel with her, locking the compartment door and pulling down the blinds. The fireman drove the train while the firing was performed by a young cleaner, who having finished the duty of 'knocker-up' was enlisted for the task. The matter reached its inevitable conclusion one day when on arrival at Huddersfield a high powered reception party was at hand, and all three were dismissed instantly. The cleaner, Charles Willie Kaye, joined the army and served with distinction and after the armistice asked to be taken back into the company's service, a request that was declined. A petition by the men of the shed on his behalf happily saw this decision reversed.

The only recipient of a commendation 'for vigilance' was Harry Eastwood who, in 1904, when working the 4.00 pm Blackpool-Leeds express entered Preston station under clear signals, but felt something was wrong. He slowed down and came to a halt when a shunting engine reversed some vans from an adjoining line, thereby averting a sidelong collision.

Whatever was written on the service record was never erased and the only features not recorded were those on disposition and political views. Strangely many drivers approaching the end of their careers, after years of unblemished service, would collect a number of cautions and reprimands. Others of the same group appeared prone to eye injuries, one of the more commonplace hazards of footplate life.

* * * * * * *

The importance of wool traffic was ingrained into everyone concerned remotely with its conveyance. Wool trains ran between Broad Street in London and Bradford (Bridge Street), where the LNWR enjoyed facilities, and ran to slick timing. The Working book indicated their conditional paths and their precedence over other traffic - which would be placed in refuge sidings to allow wool trains to overtake - so fierce was the competition for this lucrative trade.

The Bristol Wool Sales were an occasion when the LNWR operated wool buyers' specials from Bradford Exchange in competition with those operated by the Midland and Great Northern railways. The very best stock would be provided, three or four saloons and dining car and hauled by a 'Special DX' or 18 in. Goods 0-6-0 to Stockport with a conditional stop at Huddersfield. Supersonic travel had nothing on those trains, it being commonplace to reach Stockport 50 minutes after leaving Bradford and travelling via the Pickle Bridge branch between Wyke and Anchor Pit Jn. A similar engine took the train forward to Shrewsbury where it was handed over to the Great Western.

Another traffic associated with Bradford concerned theatrical trains, many of enormous length and weight and to or from places where other railways might have given a better service, e.g. Peterborough, Leicester and Carlisle. Harry Eastwood had the rare honour of receiving a half-sovereign gratuity on arrival at Liverpool (Lime Street) with such a train, the donor being the late Sir Henry Irving, the great Shakespearean actor. Goods traffic to Bradford over the L&Y

An LNWR 6 ft 0 in. 'Jumbo' on a Manchester train leaving Saddleworth station showing Saddleworth aqueduct, known locally as 'Old Sag', on the LNWR-owned Huddersfield Canal.

LNWR Society

A Leeds train arrives at Saddleworth hauled by a 'Benbow' class 4-4-0 locomotive.

LNWR Society

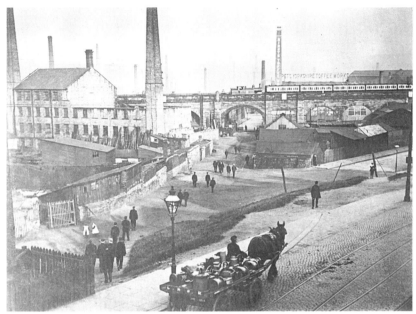

Huddersfield viaduct on 4th August, 1907 with a Leeds train hauled by a Webb 5 ft 0 in. 0-6-2 tank. The electrified Birkby tram route is in the foreground and the property beyond was acquired by the Midland Railway for its line opened in 1910.   *Revd R.G. Johnson*

usually ran via Cleckheaton or Halifax. On one occasion Joe Wigglesworth had an exhilarating run with a 'DX' 0-6-0 on a long string of empties over the Pickle Bridge line. From Wyke the line falls steeply, at 1 in 62 in one place, with numerous sharp curves and approaches the L&Y main line almost at right angles. When Wigglesworth detected his train was in two halves the prospects were frightening. Although the 'DX' was in reverse the train shot through Clifton Road like greased lighting and Wigglesworth related afterwards: 'I said my prayers but there wasn't time to make my will before we went through Anchor Pit on three wheels'.

Wigglesworth was a man of few words and many achievements. Once when working a perishables train through Standedge tunnel, a van laden with live ducks caught fire after the van body came loose on its frame. Many birds perished and it's not without significance that he afterwards observed, 'I got partial to duck - its not every day you get 'em plucked and roasted'. The name 'duck' stuck to this train and, until the early 1960s, the 4.00 pm Heaton Lodge to Ordsall Lane which ran via Manchester South Jn was known by that name.

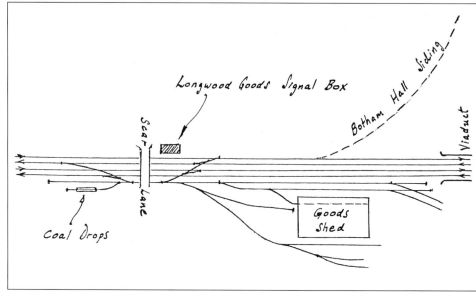

Diagram of Longwood Goods 1890.   *G.H. Brown*

The Huddersfield Joint station shunt sometime between 1919 and 1921 with, from left, on footplate Jim Hartley and Frank Cox. The shunters are Walter Hayes, Edgar Fenton, Jim Beaumont, Joe Hayes and Billy Austwick. Engine No. 235 was an 18 in. 0-6-2T.

Author's Collection

Chapter Ten

Shunting

The Hillhouse shunt link had five main jobs. The Longwood shunt was executed by a 17 in. 0-6-0 Coal Engine which in the 1920s was No. 1205, double-manned by Jack Sulch and Johnty Cooper. The former had in earlier times worked the London goods, while Cooper if I correctly recall continued to wear a tall bowler hat long after that form of headgear had vanished from the footplate. The work included the transfer of vast quantities of coal from Scarwood Sidings to Botham Hall Siding and coal drops at the back of Longwood station. At times a complete shift would be spent awaiting a clear path to bring back a string of empty wagons. Scarwood Sidings, opened in 1872, were situated to the east of Golcar station on the down side and ended before Scar Lane was reached. The site was formerly a quarry. It accommodated more than 300 wagons. Subsequently the name was used for Shaws Siding on the up side that lasted until the 1950s. Shaws owned Bottom Hall Siding on the down side which ran nearly half a mile northwards. Only the first four chains of line was LNWR-owned and the following 11 chains were owned by Shaws but maintained by the LNWR and comprised a loop. The opening of Longwood Goods yard in 1887 changed many things hereabouts. Other sidings likewise affected were Iredales Siding, to the west of Golcar Brook viaduct, and Bankhouse Siding immediately east of Slaithwaite viaduct. The former was displaced by Linthwaite Goods which opened in 1888. The depression of the 1920s changed much including more than halving the work of the shunt. Latterly a L&Y 0-6-0 saddle tank would be used which also shunted Gledholt Sidings and finished by midday.

The Huddersfield Joint station shunt was performed for six months by either company in turn. The L&Y used a Mirfield 0-6-0 saddle tank while Hillhouse used a run-down 18 in. 0-6-2 tank that had been taken off passenger duties, but whose brake power was a decided improvement over the 0-6-0 'Special Tanks'. To claim the latter's brake was poor would be a masterpiece of understatement. They often resulted in broken buffers, which in earlier times were attributed by those in authority to carelessness and fines were imposed on the driver. 'I only paid for one', recalled George Sayles, adding 'after that I had more gumption and kept a few buried in the Hillhouse embankment, just in case', these being replaced as necessary - gratis.

The two yards at Hillhouse were worked by 'Special Tanks' although the class left the shed before the Great War and did not return until 1923. Their homecoming was the outcome of firemen absenting themselves from the footplate and it was felt the need to operate the hand brake would be an inducement to stay on the job. But a way round this was found on the coal shunt. The engine would draw the train being shunted out of the yard onto the viaduct and while in such position the regulator would be opened and closed as the various cuts were made, with the hand brake wound down. The process was repeated all day long and the engine did not appear to suffer but the brake

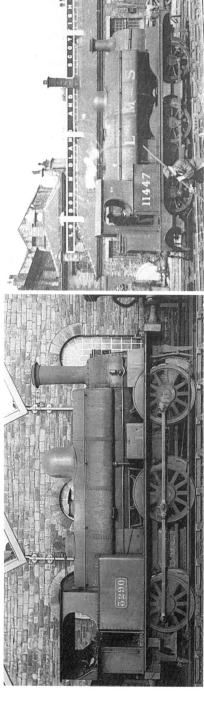

Above: The first of a trio of Hillhouse shunting engines. No. 3290 an LNWR 'Special Tank' shedded at Hillhouse between January 1926 and November 1927, when it was transferred to Longsight.
P.F. Cooke

Top right: No. 11447, an L&Y 0-6-0 saddle tank allocated between January 1938 and December 1951, when it was transferred to Mirfield.
Author's Collection

Right: No. 47403 on arrival at Hillhouse from Kingmoor on 13th September, 1955. It was transferred to York in February 1958.
Author

blocks were changed often, and being made of wood a thoughtful driver would on occasion run resin into the holes, making them more effective.

A further Coal Engine worked Heaton Lodge Sidings, the up and down yards being separated by the main line while the New Line passed outside the down yard. To all intents and purposes the sidings closed in 1932 after Mirfield Yard was opened, although actually continuing to be used to a much lesser extent than before. In 1923 no fewer than 80 guards were stationed at Heaton Lodge which gives some reflection on its importance.

The shunt link was often referred to as the 'old man link', a misnomer if there ever was one. Those taken off the main line duties for health reasons worked every bit as hard as before, some might say, even harder. Shunting backwards and forwards, stopping, reversing all day long, was a very tiresome business. The only advantages it had was that the driver was never far from home, an important factor to those whose health was indifferent. But the habits of a lifetime die hard, and not a few would have given their high teeth to have regained a place on the main line.

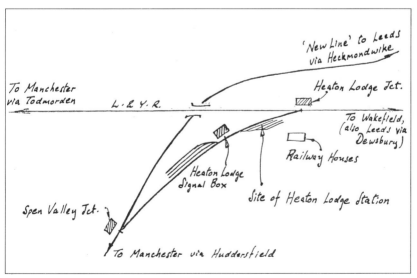

Heaton Lodge Junction 1900.   *G.H. Brown*

"The Shadowed Home."

☀ A POEM, ☀

WRITTEN BY MISS MELVEINA KERR,

Relating to the accident to Joshua Atkinson, late a fireman in the employ of the L. & N.W. Railway, Huddersfield, who was killed at Marsden Station, on December 28th, 1895, while in the execution of his duty.

He left a widow and child, for whose benefit the profits from the sale of this little work will be devoted.

PRICE TWOPENCE.

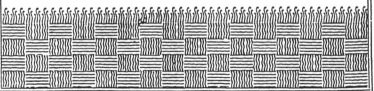

W. H. COOK, HUDD.

Chapter Eleven

Roll of Honour

Only good fortune prevented the casualty list at Hillhouse from being greater. After Jos Atkinson had been knocked down at Marsden in 1895, a 21 verse poem was written to his memory, sold at 2*d*. a copy. Proceeds went to his widow and two children.

One of the jobs in the Extra Link in 1900 included working the 4.00 pm Blackpool (Talbot Road) to Leeds New express which ran up the LNWR main line from Preston to Standish Jn, thence via Amberswood East Jn and on a short section of the Great Central track leading to Strangeways Jn, where the route converged with the Springs Branch-Eccles LNWR line. On 24th July, 1900, this train was in the charge of Fred Johnson and Alf Porter. Johnson knew the road well having worked over it regularly on goods, yet never before on a passenger train. Instead of slowing down as the Working book required, he took Amberswood East Jn at over 30 mph, came off the rails and finished up in a heap of wreckage losing his own life and that of a passenger. The Board of Trade Inquiry revealed excessive speed to be the cause, and that the Great Central track had lost some 20 per cent of its weight since being laid 14 years earlier.

A disaster occurred on 10th August, 1909 on the Micklehurst line when the leading wheels of 18 in. 0-6-2 tank No. 1608 became derailed while working a Huddersfield-Stockport express. The engine crossed a viaduct in that manner before all wheels were derailed, the engine turning over, righting itself and throwing the leading coach ahead while finishing facing in the direction it had come from. The driver, George Turton, and fireman Coates perished. The Inquiry established that the track, although in good condition, had crept outwards by some 18 inches since it was laid, thereby increasing the curve at the point of derailment. It was established that No. 1608 had been travelling at between 60 and 70 mph. The Inspecting Officer felt an engine of this type was unsuitable for such speeds, which had been a daily occurrence on many LNWR routes.

Not far away on 5th July, 1923 a Hillhouse 'Cauliflower' locomotive was involved in a terrible smash at Diggle Jn when No. 1027, manned by Ted Turner and fireman John Hutchinson, piloted a Farnley Jn 'Experiment' 4-6-0 No. 1406 with George Findlay on a Leeds to Manchester/Stockport express. This came out of the double-line Standedge tunnel, through the station and, when crossing over to the south line, collided with an L&Y 0-6-0 No. 1062 which had been shunting but was standing foul on the main line. No. 1027 turned on its side and Hutchinson, who had exchanged duties with another fireman, perished. George Findlay and a badly telescoped train finished up between the other two engines.

Accidents can occur to the most careful of men. Hudson Parker had a narrow shave on the morning of 23rd March, 1895 when he had the misfortune to obey the wrong signals at Leeds New with 4 ft 6 in. 2-4-2 tank and, leaving a platform in error, ran into North Eastern 4-4-0 No. 1531 bringing in an express from Harrogate.

"The Shadowed Home."

AN INTRODUCTION.

This little poem has been written (by request) and the object for which it is intended
is to make known the work done by the Amalgamated Society of Railway Servants, for
the widows and orphans of deceased railwaymen.

The great work of this Society is yearly increasing and worthily deserves the support
of all, as its object is to provide for the helpless and needy who have lost the support
of their homes by accident and death.

The proceeds of this poem will be given to the widow and orphan who were so
recently bereaved, to whom it is, in deep sympathy, dedicated.

Yours faithfully,

MELVEINA KERR.

'Twas in the winter of Ninety-five,
   At Christmas time, when all was gay ;
And Santa Claus took his yearly drive,
   In honour bright, at each home to stay.

The Earth's winter garment looked sad,
   Cold and bare were the fields and the grove :
But the hearts of the children were glad,
   As they clustered around the bright stove.

The homes were all brightened with holly ;
   And right goodly sounded the cheer ;
The voices so happy and jolly,
   Without even thought of a fear.

God bless all the young and the old,
   That rejoice now in innocent fun ;
Some day will the story be told,
   Of the joy and the heart sweetly won.

On the sea in the snow and the wind,
   Battling hard with the elements' power,
The lifeboat crew, noble and kind,
   Ever ready in danger's dark hour,

Went out the wrecked·crew for to save ;
   Brave, dauntlessly onward they went :
But they sank 'neath the surging wild wave.
   O'er the sea was this sad story sent.

And on the line at Marsden
   One of our townsmen stood :
Joss Atkinson, one of the firemen,
   Who was seeing if points were good.

The wind it was moaning its loudest ;
   The blinding sleet covered his face :
But he went, he was always the proudest
   To have right in every place.

He heard not approaching so quickly,
   The down goods express, as it came ;
Nor the cry of the driver, distinctly
   Calling "look out Joss ! mind, there's the train."

It flew past and on in its fury;
   They knew not, when driving the train,
That a life had been taken most surely,
   By the steel hearted rail horse again.

The driver then looked for the signal
   The lantern's bright eye should have sent:
" All's right mate, go ahead, it is well."
He then jumped from his engine and went

To see what the man was about ;
   " Oh ! God ! is it true ? " he exclaimed,
When he saw *life's* bright lamp had gone out ;
   That his comrade by *death* had been claimed.

Then let us our tribute now pay,
   And honour the brave and the true,
Who for duty and honour, to-day
   The portals of death have passed through.

Many heroes shine in battlefields of war ;
   And triumph on the sea amid the storm ;
But brave and noble men are found on shore,
   Who drive the powerful iron horse's form.

When danger comes their courage never fails,
   And oft' they give both limb and life,
To save the lives they carry on the rails ;
   Thus many noble heroes close their earthly strife.

A shadow was falling in gloom,
   O'er a home where bright sunshine had reigned ;
So cheerful and bright was the room
   That love in its triumph had gained.

A mother was watching her baby,
   Wee innocent, smiling so sweet,
As she told it to clap for dear daddy,
   And look for his coming to greet.

Alas ! for that mother and baby ;
   Who dare to her carry the tale ;
But gently they told her for daddy
   The baby, wee darling, would wail.

For he had gone home unto glory,
   And never could see them here more ;
God only can soften the story,
   When they meet on the heavenly shore.

He surely will comfort the widow,
   And soothe the poor orphan's cry ;
And bless those who kindness do show,
   To all the bereaved ones who sigh.

They need our help in their trouble,
   Our sympathy in their deep grief ;
And God will repay you all double,
   Who send to the needy relief.

M. Melveina Kerr.

The aftermath of the Amberswood East Jn derailment in which a Hillhouse driver and fireman lost their lives.
Author's Collection

The Railway Clearing House 1912 junction of diagram showing the layout of lines in the Amberswood area.

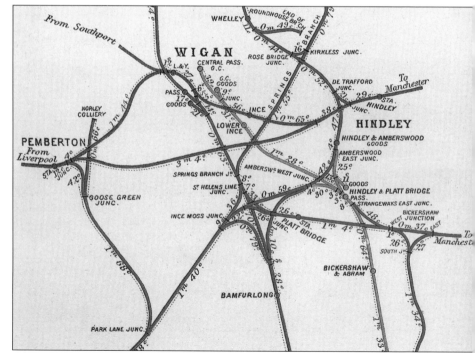

Derailment of L&YR 0-6-0 saddle tank No. 547 on 6th April, 1908. Shunting here, as at Huddersfield was done for six months alternately. LNWR locomotive foreman James Goulding can be clearly seen in his bowler hat.   *Author's Collection*

The scene at Friezland on 10th August, 1909. The engine was derailed after it had run with its leading driving wheels on top of the rails, it then was completely derailed and finished up facing the down direction from which it had just come, throwing the first coach ahead of it.
                                                                              Author's Collection

The collision on 7th October, 1910 at Heckmondwike L&YR station between an LNWR Coal Engine and empty wagons.   *Author's Collection*

The Diggle Disaster of 5th July, 1923 with LNWR 18 in. Goods No. 1027 lying across the tracks after collision with L&YR 0-6-0 No. 1062. The 18 in. Goods was piloting 'Experiment' class No. 1406 *George Findlay*. Both Hillhouse men perished.   *Author's Collection*

The following list speaks for itself. Not all men were killed but a large number sustained injuries causing them to leave the footplate.

Joseph Parker	Accidentally killed 1866
Thomas Ashton	Aged 20, killed 14.12.1866 attempting to couple engine to fresh tender
Jos Atkinson	Aged 30, killed Marsden 28.12.1895 attempting to change points in extreme weather conditions
Fred Johnson (37) and Alf Porter	Killed Amberswood East Jn 27.4.1900 when train derailed at speed
Jos Megson and David Senior	Injured in collision at Birmingham (New Street) with Midland train on 2nd August, 1903
W. Turton and J. Coates	Killed Friezland in September 1909 after engine derailed at speed on Stockport Express
Gladstone Cocking (46)	Killed Holmes Chapel on 25th January, 1914 after his head struck a bridge
Ambrose Leeming	Knocked down at Hillhouse No. 1 in 1916 and lost a leg. Became lampman.
Jack Hutchinson (23)	Formerly of Warrington killed at Diggle Jn on 5th July, 1923 in double-headed collision with shunting engine
Josh Woods	Killed Hillhouse No. 1 after fall from engine June 1930
R.A. Martin	Killed at Golcar in April 1935 after fall from engine
A.E. Hirst	Killed 6th June, 1935 aged 55
S.H.F. Neville	Stalled in single line-tunnel at Standedge in 1953 with No. 45501 *St Dunstan's*. Train emerged two hours later. On 29th March, 1956 drove No. 42384 into a train of coaches at Clayton West. Lost front of foot when run over by an 'Austerity' 2-8-0 in 1962 at Hillhouse Shed.
D. Eddon	Fireman in Clayton West mishap on 29th March, 1956
Lawrence Campbell and Russell Sykes	Manning the Liverpool-Stockport Mail on 18th January, 1964 they collided at Broadheath after a preceding goods had been erroneously set back on the line they used. Both miraculously survived. Engine No. 45695 *Minotaur* (55C) was cut up. By a strange coincidence the locomotive that had been used on this train during the preceding week was No. 45708 *Resolution* which that morning had been dispatched to Crewe for scrapping. No. 45695 having received a general overhaul at Crewe was on its first day's work since returning to Farnley Shed.

BR No. 49501 derailed at Meltham in 1949.
Author's Collection

No. 42384 reposes on Hillhouse Shed after running out of control and into a train of empty stock at Clayton West on 20th March, 1956.   *Author's Collection*

Farnley Jn 'Jubilee' class 4-6-0 No. 45695 *Minotaur* after the Broadheath collision on 18th January, 1964 when crewed by Hillhouse men driver Laurie Campbell and fireman Russell Sykes on a Liverpool (Lime Street) to Stockport mail train.   *Author's Collection*

Chapter Twelve

Utterly Dedicated

If anyone at Hillhouse Shed could justly be described as an utterly dedicated driver, John Armitage fitted this description, for driving was more than a matter of occupation, it was his whole life.

Armitage began his career as a junior clerk at Slaithwaite, this gave him little satisfaction and he received his calling to the Locomotive Department six months later. Starting at Hillhouse on 20th October, 1900 as a cleaner he was paid 9s. for a week of 54 hours, walking seven miles to work as a regular habit when on early turn. 'I had three fights on my first day', he used to recall, adding, 'after that I never had a wrong word with anyone!'

On nights he was often required to spend much of his shift as a 'knocker-up', for that was the name given to the person sent out to waken those whose duty was to book on at the shed at some unearthly time during the night. Both driver and fireman, perhaps living up to three miles apart, had to be wakened. Armed with a long stick, a bedroom window would be tapped until acknowledged, or if the height were too great small lumps of earth or pebbles would be thrown. The job had its frustrations, for example when standing outside a house and making enough noise to waken the whole neighbourhood, yet competing with the effects of a stimulating beverage consumed only a few hours earlier. As 'knocker-up' Armitage knew all the short cuts through snickets and passages or across back gardens and allotments, saving a few minutes walk and punctuated by a short nap on the warm flags outside a bakery, or beneath a shop verandah that gave refuge in foul weather. He also learnt a thing or two about those he was sent to waken, but that is another story.

Promoted to fireman in May 1907, he then worked a 60 hour week with 10 hour shifts firing for Henry Cox on a shunting engine: Hillhouse Top Yard, Hillhouse Low Yard, Heaton Lodge, Huddersfield Goods and the Longwood shunt.

Armitage quickly worked his way through all the links and by the time the Great War began was driving regularly whenever required. During the war Hillhouse had requests for volunteers to work weekends at Crewe. Thus it became his habit to travel to London, Peterborough, Holyhead, Carlisle, Swansea and a host of other places - he would tackle any work whether he knew the road or not. Frequently when booking on, it was assumed that he was the fireman doing the job for the driver. When asked, 'Does your driver know the route?' he would reply in the affirmative without giving the information that he himself was the driver!

Sometimes after such work he would not reach home until halfway through the following week. On one such occasion, while travelling 'on the cushions' from Stafford to Crewe, he placed his double-trip basket on the opposite seat in the front compartment in which he was riding. At Norton Bridge an elderly gentleman and his wife boarded the train, and Armitage moved his belongings to the luggage rack, but the movement of the train loosened the stopper on a bottle of cocoa and presently he noticed a steady flow of drops falling on to the old gentleman's silk top hat. He thought that they looked a nice couple but his opinion changed when the lady saw what had happened, and before the situation could be remedied, a disturbance took place - to put it mildly. At Crewe, the lady sent for the station master, but seizing the opportunity Armitage and his mate slipped out into the night!

Appointed a regular driver in 1920, his first job was on a shunting engine, but shortly afterwards he exchanged places with someone in the Extra Link and in this capacity travelled to many distant places on excursions, theatrical specials, banana trains, pigeon specials and the snow plough in winter. In fact he would work any kind of train, with any load to any destination. During the summer months earnings could be very high with much of the day spent on the move, but in winter earnings could be reduced to a pittance.

Should the Micklehurst line become blocked by snow all resources would be transferred to keep the adjacent Greenfield line open. During 1917, working a goods towards Huddersfield, he stopped for signals between Micklehurst and Freizland and remained there because the line ahead had become blocked. After standing there seven hours, he had to drop the fire when all the water had been used up. Engine and train remained where it was until the weather improved.

In the early days of Grouping he took an excursion train to Blackpool using the L&Y route via Brighouse, Copy Pit and Accrington. On the return he was delayed at Bamber Bridge and observed a Fleetwood fish train appear and saunter ahead of him. From here onwards he was checked from one signal to the next and eventually was shouted at by an enraged passenger. In due course the train pulled up at Rose Grove to await the fish train which ambled past after travelling via the Padiham loop. At this point he looked over the side of the engine and told the signalman 'what I thought about the Lanky' - the signalman in reply then 'told me what he thought about the Wessie'. Although never formally meeting, a strong friendships often sprung from an introduction by such means.

About this time No. 2222 *Sir Gilbert Claughton* sustained a minor failure and after repair was appropriated by Hillhouse Shed. It gave Armitage considerable pleasure to use this engine for a whole week on the morning Halifax-Stockport train. On another occasion, while seated in the chair of his local barber, the hairdresser related how over the previous weekend he had travelled to Glasgow on a special train. On the return, after a frustrating start, the train made a meteoric journey between Beattock and Preston, apparently being 'driven down Shap by a madman'. Armitage listened with great interest and no little amusement but made no comment, except to enquire if the homecoming had been safe and punctual, without adding that he was the 'madman' referred to!

During the late 1920s a new foreman at Edgeley Shed, Stockport, started a practice of relieving train crews with men from his own shed, where at the time there was a shortage of work. This occurred a number of times to the 9.20 pm Hillhouse-London goods. On this particular occasion as Armitage was taking water, two men appeared from out of the dark with the message 'We've been sent to relieve you, the foreman wants you at the shed'.

Knowing this would mean returning home, 'on the cushions' and losing money, Armitage merely nodded and left the fresh crew to finish taking water. When this had been done, Armitage and his mate reappeared alongside the engine and shouted to the Edgeley men, 'Your foreman has just given me a message that you are to report back to the shed - and from the way he said it, he wants you there in a hurry'. Thus the uninvited returned from where they had come and Armitage and his fireman carried on to where they had set out for. He was an excellent man to work with and a demon to travel behind. He used to chuckle, 'I've often been booked for going too fast, but never for going too slow'. A young fireman would learn quickly, if he were willing to be taught, for Armitage treated those under him with great understanding.

Many records of Armitage's locomotive exploits exist, the following being typical. When No. 13118 was newly built and working the 1.18 pm Huddersfield-Crewe, the first seven miles from starting on a 1 in 96 gradient at Huddersfield to passing Marsden on a gradient averaging 1 in 105 took 10 minutes and 8 seconds. The load however was modest, a mere three ex-L&Y non-corridor coaches. Until the Trans-Pennine diesels came 30 years later it was a record not easily bettered. Armitage had a high opinion of the 'Crabs' when new or fresh after overhaul. Of the Black Staniers No. 5005 was his favourite, but others would claim No. 5061 to be superior. His use of a new or unfamiliar type of engine became a challenge to his enginemanship, first getting to know it then coaxing it to do the work, with the result that his opinion and criticism of such engines was always fair and constructive. It would be no exaggeration to say that he became a legend in his own lifetime. He claimed with some pride and justification to know and to have travelled over almost every mile on the LNWR.

On his retirement in 1950 he became a much sought-after speaker who held his audience under a spell for two hours without either notes or visual aids. His leisure time was devoted to voluntary unpaid public duties. Elected a Labour Councillor in 1936, he became an Alderman 10 years later. Appointed a Justice of the Peace in 1945 he became Mayor of Huddersfield during 1954/55 making history as the town's first railwayman so honoured. In this respect he was emulated by two other Hillhouse men, Alderman R.H. Browne and Alderman J.A. Bray, who were respectively driver and fitter.

Alderman Jack Armitage   Alderman Harry Browne,   Alderman J.A. Bray
                              twice Mayor of Huddersfield.

Bill Elson stands alongside diesel-mechanical shunter No. D2173 at Huddersfield on return from Stockport having worked a scratch special on 29th April, 1967, the day before his retirement.

Author

Chapter Thirteen

Miscellaneous Memories

Aaron Sharrett and the Crewe Job

Crewe North Shed had one regular passenger duty to Huddersfield all the year round. This locomotive arrived on the 12.05 am ex-Crewe down Mail in the small hours, the 6 ft 6 in. 'Jumbo' becoming the last engine to go on shed. It was also the last engine to leave the shed later the same night. The train was worked between Huddersfield and Normanton, where it terminated, by L&Y men and engines until 1902 when it was diverted to Leeds New station, the Crewe North men taking it through and handing over to the North Eastern who worked it to York.

Aarron Sharrett was a regular driver of this train over many years. His career contained a crop of mishaps, including running into the back of George Mossley in Huddersfield tunnel after missing a signal due to heavy smoke. This was on 24th October, 1883 when Mossley was banking a goods train that had stalled due to shortage of steam. No story is more worthy of repetition than an occurrence in 1904, when as he backed down onto the up Mail at Leeds, his fireman received a serious hand injury and was taken to the Infirmary. The Mail was due out within minutes. As no relief fireman could be found in so short a time, a porter was persuaded to travel on the footplate and a promise given that a fresh fireman would be waiting his arrival at Huddersfield. Here, Sharrett looked down from the cab of No. 1905 *Black Diamond*, a Webb 'Jubilee' compound, to observe a small youth clad in fireman's clothes, who it transpired was just 16 and had never fired before. Sharrett placing one hand on either side of the lad's waist, lifted him up, and after some contemplation put him down on the opposite side of the cab telling him 'it would be best if you kept out of the way'. Having driven and fired all the way from Leeds he continued to Crewe in such manner, where he asked his youthful spectator, 'What do you think to being a fireman?' and received the reply, 'Alright - it's a better job than yours!'

Bill Elson

The career of this man might form a book on its own. A Salop man, he worked at Coleham Shed and was later outstationed at Clee Hill where the LNWR had a very isolated sub-shed. In 1922 he was made redundant and moved to Hillhouse along with 28 men from other depots. In later years employed only on goods work, when the shed became dieselised he was but five months before retirement. Untrained on the English Electric Type '4s' he was put on a job of his own with a 204 hp Drewry shunter. His penultimate day's work was preceded the previous night by a serious derailment at Leeds City which caused the main air supply for all points to fracture. The Up Mail (York to Shrewsbury TPO) was

Instruction coaches were regular visitors. Here an LNWR 12-wheel saloon is seen after being used on Locomotive Improvement class duties, along with a similar vehicle used for St John's Ambulance Brigade class training. From 1938 other vehicles were used for ARP instruction. The last such train to visit comprised DE320043, DE951650 (clerestory) and DE961800. *W.B. Stocks*

A Webb compound 4 cylinder 4-6-0 No. 1466 at Farnley Jn Shed in 1903.   *Author's Collection*

cancelled; the following morning a scratch train was assembled with five vehicles and Bill was the only man available to take this train to Stockport Edgeley (taking 1 hour and 50 minutes). So the one time Bangor Mail got through and Elson returned home light engine in triumphant style with engine No. D2173. The date was 29th April, 1967 with retirement due the next day.

Frequent Visitors

A pair of old coaches were suitably modified for use for the Locomotive Improvement Class and included locomotive valve gear etc. These vehicles were the most frequent visitors to the shed, coming with a cinema coach and were stabled in No. 1 road and steam heated. Next in frequency were visits by a First Aid train, again with cinema coach and just before World War II, an LMS Air Raid Precautions train and cinema coach, both painted yellow. In each case a compartment for the instructor would be retained. The frequency with which such visits were made showed how well abreast of the times the LMS was. The ARP coach gave demonstrations in many places to other railway staff. In every case the overall theme was to improve railwaymen's confidence in what it they might be faced with. No industrial concern compared with the thoroughness of this training. The picture taken in bay No. 3 at Huddersfield station about 1950 (*opposite*) shows the location chosen as the site of the 1957 new signal box. On 3rd December, 1963 the instruction train appeared on shed for the last time and comprised DE320043, 951650 (clerestory) and 961800.

The London Goods

The 9.20 pm Hillhouse-London goods was the best-known train to operate from the West Riding, by whose punctuality watches were set. At the end of 1903 a couple of Webb 4-cylinder compound 4-6-0 goods locomotives arrived for this duty. No. 1400 was Jack Sulch's engine while No. 1466, which earlier had been at Farnley Jn, was used by Fred Townend. The train was worked to Basford Hall Sidings, Crewe. In 1905 No. 606 joined them on this work but from 1907 the newly-built 19 in. 4-6-0 goods engines became responsible, being ousted by new 'G1s' by 1914, by which time the train was worked only as far as Stockport Edgeley. In November 1921 No. 2592 was outstationed at Low Moor L&Y shed to work the train, at that time starting its journey at Bradford (Bridge Street). For a time Harry Eastwood was on this duty and on one occasion No. 2592 sustained a big end failure in Bowling tunnel. This was stripped down and disconnected before continuing to Hillhouse on one cylinder!

In Jack Armitage's time both engine and men worked through to London (Broad Street). The 'Prince of Wales' superheater 4-6-0s were assigned to this duty, including No. 331 and 889 both Belpaire fitted. The greatest change took place in the summer of 1934 when two new Stanier 2-6-0s arrived. These were Nos. 13278/9, but the width over their cylinders caused problems when working over North Stafford lines in the Churnet Valley and resulted in

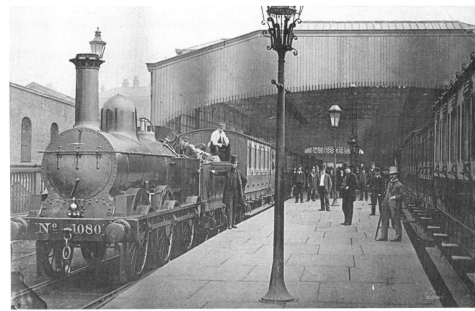

LNWR 'DX Goods' 0-6-0 No. 1080 at Manchester Victoria after 1868. This class was used on all types of traffic including Hillhouse to London goods when inaugurated. The picture is often said to have been taken by G.T. Rhodes.   *Author's Collection*

A much travelled and most unusual allocation. 'Minnie' looks down from the footplate of 'WD' No. 90694 on 18th May, 1966.   *Author*

replacement by Fowler engines. One of these, No. 2729 driven by Joe Lawton, was involved in an accident at Roade Jn near Rugby.

In May 1948 Stanier class '5s' took over when Nos. 44780 and 44948/9 were delivered to the shed. These engines performed consistently with other engines of the same class. The diagrammed working began in the traditional way with the 9.20 pm Hillhouse to Camden. On the second day the engine came north on a Euston-Blackpool express which it worked to Crewe, where it then took over a Crewe to Colne express. It returned the third day to Stockport with through coaches from Colne to Euston, the engine returning to its home shed on a goods from Adswood to Mirfield.

In August 1957 the diagram was transferred to Rose Grove Shed, the engines also being moved there, but it made little difference, although in the early 1960s the duty was taken over by Crewe South Shed and finally by Stoke, by which time the train began its journey at Healey Mills. Change is the law of life and the 8.50 pm Healey Mills-London goods ran for the last time on 31st August, 1966.

Jack Sulch enjoyed telling a story of how, as a young fireman working this train during the 1880s with a rundown 'DX' 0-6-0 goods, he had a sharp exchange of words with its driver. George Prestwick was a proud, upstanding figure to whom the idea of asking for a fresh engine would be the height of degradation. Noting how little co-operation he received one day when the weather was both raining and humid and not having had the shovel out of his hand for a great distance, Sulch straightened his back to observe his mate peering out over the spectacle plate through a haze of steam with the rain running off the end of his beard. He exclaimed, 'I wish I was a driver', whereupon Prestwick replied, 'I'll tell you summat - I wish were t'guard'.

No account of Hillhouse Shed would be complete without mentioning its most unusual allocation - Minnie the messroom cat. A grey mottled tabby of rare pedigree, she could mount the footplate in one leap with ease. Once aboard she would walk through the tender and rest on the tender tank. In this way Minnie was almost transferred, for on 18th August, 1965 she was aboard No. 44829 when it left for Healey Mills to work the 8.50 pm Healey Mills-London goods (the old 9.20 Hillhouse-London goods in modern guise). She was not discovered until water was taken on the Standedge water troughs, where in a somewhat bedraggled state she hauled herself over the coal into the arms of a surprised crew. They made her comfortable by placing her in a carton for return from Edgeley on the footplate of No. 48437!

Ex-Government Locomotives

Early in 1920 several of the Robinson-designed 2-8-0s were received on loan from the Ministry of Munitions. These were used on heavy goods working, coal trains and frequently with coke trains to Mold Jn. Surprisingly, for what was an alien design, they were well liked - a unique compliment for an engine designed by another company.

Regrettably they received only the barest mechanical attention, although the only trouble that arose was with the Westinghouse brake pump. The trouble

No. 2052, the first of the Great Central designed engines loaned from the Ministry of Munitions after World War I. *Author*

was 'cured' by giving the affected mechanism a hearty clout with a pick axe shaft - the real cause however was lack of lubrication. The first one to arrive on shed was No. 2052 which was placed at the top of No. 8 road. The fitters spent two whole days before they managed to get the brakes off! Many firemen have vivid recollections of having to go over the side of the engine as it gathered speed down a gradient, walk along the footplate and clout the pump. No doubt many guards will also have cause to remember being thrown from one end of the brake van to the other when the engine's brakes were applied.

A Locomotive Exchange - 1921 Duties

The different links in 1921 were:

Passenger	Express
	Bulldog 18 in. 0-6-2 tank
	5 ft 6 in. 2-4-2 tank
	Kirkburton 4 ft 6 in. 2-4-2 tank motor fitted
Goods	Goods
	Coal
	Double Trip
	Trip and Shunt links
	Extra Link

In addition there were various individuals who not only had their own particular engine, but their own individual duties. Johnty Cooper for example, finished his time on the Kirkheaton Ballast shunt* using No. 1205, a Webb 0-6-0 Coal Engine. This involved collecting and disposing of all engine ashes from Hillhouse and Farnley Jn Sheds, Copley Hill Yard and Leeds Central station and as far west as Ash Bridge, Oldham, Stalybridge, etc.

In this year a small exchange of engines took place between Hillhouse and Wakefield sheds, the former receiving No. 138, a L&Y 'C1' class, No. 23 an 0-6-0 saddle tank and No. 427, a class '27' 0-6-0. Wakefield in exchange received Nos. 109 and 774, a pair of 18 in. 'Cauliflowers'. The stay of the latter was brief after someone lit up without first filling the boiler: perhaps someone on the L&Y thought this the quickest way to return borrowed property.

A recurring habit of footplatemen would be to greet the appearance of a new or unfamiliar type with a critical eye. All Midland engines and most of those from the L&Y suffered in this respect, while the improvements conspicuous on modern engines, cab refinements, improved brake, regulator handle, seat, overall protection from weather, etc. were scornfully dismissed. It was only in retrospect that justice was belatedly done, yet one of the doubtful and quite misleading features introduced was the Midland power classification for all types after Grouping. To designate the Webb 5 ft 6 in. 2-4-2 tanks as '1P' was ridiculous. In 1923 a large-boilered 0-8-0 from Mirfield Shed was tried on the London goods, but was neither able to haul the load, maintain speed nor keep time as difficulty was experienced in maintaining steam. This class, known as 'Moriahs', was never popular with LNWR men.

There were but four locomotive inspectors on the whole of the LNWR, holding a rank on a par with locomotive foremen. At this time these comprised Messrs Jackson of Rugby, Davis of Chester, Chalmers of Carlisle and Dick Gore of Edge Hill. When the latter retired Fred Townend of Hillhouse succeeded Dick Gore as locomotive inspector at Edge Hill *c*. 1920.

Small and Narrow

Diggle and Marsden owe much to the canal and railway tunnels for their development. In 1890 the LNWR commenced work making its own double-line tunnel, and until 1893, when this task was handed over to three foremen who became contractors, a 2 ft 6 in. 0-4-0 well tank shunter was employed to convey men and materials to the workface. It reposed in its own short bay at the end of the down north platform at Diggle afterwards, before being returned to Crewe.

Between 1914 and 1918 when Tunnel End reservoir was being rehabilitated, a 2 ft 6 in. tramway was laid on the towpath of the Huddersfield Canal, extending about one mile from Tunnel End to Warehouse Hill. Trains of sludge were conveyed for tipping at the eastern extremity before returning to Marsden goods yard, entered after reversal, and emerging loaded with puddle clay for transit to the reservoir. Two trains of clay per day originating at Micklehurst were

---

* Kirkheaton Ballast tip embraced a large slope that gradually was levelled off over the years with an estimated 4 million tons of engine ash. It was used regularly until 1953, by which time the layout of the siding had changed every few years. Circus trains visiting Huddersfield were subsequently accommodated here to clean out the stock, the last time one such train ran it was taken through to Kirkburton in 1957.

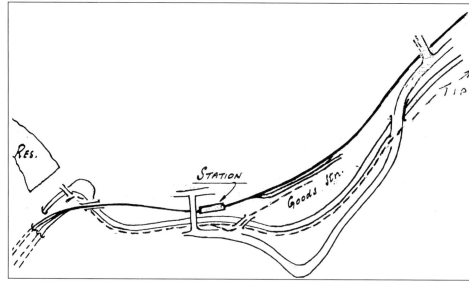

Diagram of Light Railway laid along canal towpath at Marsden during cleaning out of Tunnel End Reservoir.   *G.H. Brown*

LNWR narrow gauge locomotive *Platelayer* on the Huddersfield Canal towpath at Marsden with its crew, E. Munt (*left*) and W. Denby (*right*).   *Author's Collection*

operated for this purpose, being hauled by 0-6-0 Coal Engines. The three locomotives of the LNWR Engineering Department used were quite unlike any other possessed by the company. *Jim Crow* and *Platelayer* had painted names while *Kitchener* a more sophisticated engine, boasted a proper cab and cast nameplate with raised lettering. All three were accommodated in a wooden shed erected at Warehouse Hill, where they were maintained by Hillhouse personnel.

The engines details were as follows:

Platelayer	W.G. Bagnall 1410 (1892)
Jim Crow	Hudswell, Clarke 340 (1894)
Kitchener	W.G. Bagnall 1999 (1914)

The General Strike (1926)

Two of the few duties performed at Hillhouse Shed during the Strike were worked by two railway enthusiast brothers, both volunteers. John and Paddy Hirst* served as firemen on a couple of 19 in. goods 4-6-0s, John on No. 1630 and Paddy on No. 2619. These had been prepared and left shed coupled tender to tender. At Huddersfield they were uncoupled before receiving the attention of Mr Brereton the station master; a portly figure, it was his task to attend to the signalling, the magnitude of which is measured when it is explained that the two Huddersfield cabins, both elevated and approached by ladders, were at extreme ends of the station, in fact Huddersfield No. 2 was 150 yards beyond the platform ramp. Once coupled to their respective trains one locomotive would run to Manchester, where after reversal it would run through to Leeds before returning home. The second engine did exactly the same but in the reverse order.

On the first day, it had been announced on the infant wireless that the Manchester train would call at all stations, whereas instructions had been given to run non-stop beyond Stalybridge. At Ashton the platform was packed as the train sped through, only to make an unscheduled stop at Clayton Bridge after running through the crossing gates. As stated earlier, on the Kirkburton branch only one train ran, hauled by 18 in. 0-6-2 tank No. 189 which, however, had its fire dropped at the terminus, having left from Huddersfield without sufficient water.

'Experiments' and 'Princes'

Just after the arrival of 'Experiment' class 4-6-0 No. 165 *City of Lichfield*, George Rolls Stocks used that engine on a Saturday holiday train from Leeds to Blackpool, calling at all intermediate (New Line) stations to Huddersfield. His fireman was Harry Mellor who had arranged to meet his newly-married wife early that evening on finishing duty. But the footplate is no respecter of private life and hopes of fulfilling this appointment were shattered when, waiting return from Blackpool, they were directed to back down, not onto the Leeds train, but another. In a moment a whistle was blown and a flag waved without either Stocks or Mellor being aware of the train's destination. Enquiries produced the

* John and Paddy Hirst were both long serving members of the Stephenson Locomotive Society.

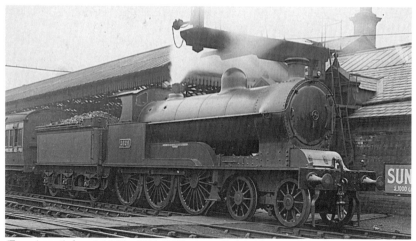

'Experiment' class 4-6-0 No. 2626 *Chillington* at Stalybridge on a Manchester Exchange to Leeds train. This engine came to Hillhouse in March 1923 and stayed until April 1934, but the last four years were spent in store. Driver Ellis Rowley can be seen on the footplate.

P.F. Cooke

reply: 'First stop Crewe'! In due course it was discovered the train was bound for Birmingham and as no relief crew was evident at Crewe, they would be expected to work through. But instead of returning from Birmingham 'on the cushions' they were ordered to book off and return at 10.00 pm. Ultimately they reached home midway through the next morning after working a theatrical special to Manchester. Such was an engineman's way of life at that period.

Stocks had a quality of rough-hewn grandeur, and he made his work look easy. Ben Garner, never a man to scatter compliments carelessly, once described his firing as 'the nearest thing possible to a mechanical stoker', due to his capacity to shovel coal into the firebox. As a driver he would readily assist his fireman, as he did with Harry Mellor on 'Prince of Wales' No. 745 *Pluto* on a Saturday in 1924 on the evening Crewe-Halifax train. Owing to an engine failure on the 'Sunny South Express' he was called upon to take out a train of 16 coaches and ran the 17 miles from Crewe to the first stop at Alderley Edge in 21 minutes, exactly as booked. Joe Lawton, a speed merchant in the same era, thought nothing of coming over the New Line from Leeds with a 'Prince' and eight on in 24 minutes non-stop to Huddersfield. It was on a day when he had charge of LMS No. 5714 (old No. 1351) on the 3.45 pm Liverpool (Lime Street)-Hull buffet car train, that a delay occurred before the train had started its journey. Lawton cut the schedule to such purpose that he didn't shut off soon enough before taking the curves between Orsdall Lane and Manchester Exchange, and as a result a passenger in the buffet car was covered with a trayful of hot food. Six weeks later, on the same duty, the guard at Liverpool, when informing him of the train's weight, chided '. . . tons - and mind the gravy'!

Train Operations

A bad start and slipping could cause broken couplings and the danger of run-backs. Good running meant co-operation with the guard, the correct use of the whistle, each siding or junction having its own whistle code. First a whistle to the guard to screw down his hand brake, then the fireman would screw down the tender hand brake while locomotive would be put in reverse and steam applied. Varying weather conditions had to be taken into account and effective braking would be assisted by how much coal and water the tender contained and the gradient. It was usual on nearing a summit for the driver to whistle for the guard to apply his brake and the train passed over the top with couplings taut. If the guard did not comply, the handling of an unbraked goods could become a nightmare.

Driving was a job that called for great skill and nerves of iron. A train coming down an incline could become divided and the remedial measures taken by the driver and guard were imperative if disaster was to be avoided - assessing the situation to bring the two loose portions together without impact.

The steam brake and iron brake blocks used in later years produced an element of certainty as never known before. The Clark and Webb chain brake was in its day regarded as a good brake, the guard winding a windlass to tighten up the chain linkages. But if the linkage broke, the brake vanished. Overloading was common and trains often divided, the second portion being taken up afterwards, but the idea of asking for assistance was rare; for this to occur on a main line would result in an inquiry.

The universal method of stopping was for an engine to be placed in reverse gear and steam applied, with the effect not unlike that of a jet engine using reverse thrust when landing - but the knock-on effect caused steam to leak from the front end. After a time the escape became so prominent that the engine was continuously enveloped in steam. A good example to recall is the ex-LNWR 0-8-0s restarting from Huddersfield's up goods loop. After a time, when the locomotive had been washed out, a fitter known as the joint maker would give attention to eliminate all unnecessary waste of steam. This involved slackening all the nuts around the front end and applying new packing before tightening up.

The practice of stopping on the reversing screw was used by older drivers and was still fashionable in the early 1940s. The LMS Black Staniers and ex-L&Y 0-6-0 saddle tanks were great performers in this respect. In about 1985 I spoke with a retired Patricroft driver who recalled that, on the eve of the demise of the LNWR 'G2s' about 1961, he was working a westbound heavy tank train down the bank from Miles Platting. Speed began to increase beyond the 8 mph which he considered the correct speed for the gradient: he then placed the engine in reverse, applied steam, and reached the foot of the bank safely.

A 5 ft 6 in. 2-4-2T No. 2265 allocated to Hillhouse from November 1923 until September 1929 when it was withdrawn. It is seen here painted in LMS crimson lake livery and numbered 6732 - the first Hillhouse engine so painted.   *P.F. Cooke*

The L&Y 2-4-2 radial tanks were successors to the LNWR 5 ft 6 in. 2-4-2 tanks. Here No. 10946, a superheated engine was allocated from October 1934 until December 1940.

Author's Collection

Chapter Fourteen

The Years of Change and the Last Days

In the five year period between Grouping and 1928, Hillhouse Shed showed little visible change of ownership. A large number of men redundant at other ex-LNWR depots arrived, 29 in total being added to the strength of the shed but dislocating the seniority hopes of those had worked at Hillhouse longer. Some of the duties hitherto undertaken by the former L&Y passed to Hillhouse and included trains to Meltham and Holmfirth and to Halifax and Bradford, while excursions to Blackpool regularly worked via Bradley Wood and Rose Grove.

Few LNWR engines had acquired LMS-type numerals, but one day all those not renumbered were dealt with in the space of a few hours. The old number plates were discarded and small white stencilled numbers substituted. When the shed passed into the LMS Central Division nearly all the small engines allocated were replaced by ex-L&Y types, but tradition dies hard and the newcomers were viewed with mixed feelings. On the whole some good results were achieved, although a few of the L&Y 'A' class 0-6-0s were found to be shy steamers - a remedy for which was to work the engine hard uphill and hold a shovelful of sand in the firebox door. The sand was sucked over the brick arch and through the tubes where it removed any obstruction before coming out of the chimney like shotblast! Tank engines were invariably used on short distance work, the longer runs being monopolised by tender engines. Those to whom the scene beforehand was unknown would find it difficult to reconcile the regular use of a 5 ft 6 in. 2-4-2 tank working to Liverpool on the Mail, or to Hull after some failure, but this had been the usual thing.

The arrival of the Hughes 2-6-0s in 1930 was a landmark, being the first LMS design allocated and some really amazing speeds were achieved on passenger work. Of the goods duties taken over from the L&Y was one known as 'the drummer' which involved working coal from Clayton West. The 'Super Ds' lifted 32 loaded wagons out of the bottom from Park Mill Colliery through Skelmanthorpe up to Clayton West Jn, but at times of bad weather some breathtaking journeys followed downhill to Springwood Jn, even though wagons brakes were pinned down. The arrival of the Black Staniers saw unfavourable comparison made with the 'Prince of Wales' class they superseded, yet when the men came to know the new engines, sparks began to fly. Bertie Willie was reputed to have run the 5.25 pm from Leeds to Liverpool via the New Line to a dead stand for signals at Hillhouse No. 2 in 18½ minutes with No. 5061 - it was said the crossover at Spen Valley Jn was straightened out in the process! Bert Whalley came down the bank from Howley Park at high speed on the morning Hull-Liverpool express hauled by No. 5005 and, approaching Dewsbury, discovered to his horror that, instead of being signalled to pass through the station on the platform line as was usual, he was routed via the main through road, which began with a sharp bend. Everyone aboard that day held the belief that as they passed through Dewsbury an earth tremor was taking place. The through road, right until its removal in 1963, had a very rough reputation.

An up excursion passing Longwood and Milnsbridge in 1935 hauled by Nos. 8435 and 12257.
Cyril Whitaker

An excursion to Blackpool about to leave Holmfirth station hauled by Stanier 'Black Five' No. 45210 on 14th August, 1952.
Author

Double trips and lodging turns gradually disappeared during World War II. To compensate for the discontinuance of the Halifax-Euston through coaches, a brand new service between Huddersfield and Wakefield Westgate was introduced as from 21st September, 1953. Throughout its existence ex-L&Y 2-4-2 tanks and two ex-LMS corridors would be used on this service which made connection with Leeds Central-King Cross expresses. The outward trip was in the morning with an evening return, the engine involved being utilised to make a round trip between Normanton and Sowerby Bridge.

Some of the locomotive highlights on this roster include the use of 4-4-0 No. 40680 (27D) on 5th April, 1956, having arrived at Hillhouse the previous day *en route* to Farnley Jn on transfer. Fowler 2-6-4 tanks would be substituted in case of failure, other engines used include 0-6-0 No. 44409 on 8th August, 1956, while on 22nd November, 1956 Aspinall 2-4-2T No. 50865 failed at Brighouse and was replaced by Sowerby Bridge 2-6-4 tank No. 42151. Similarly the same engine failed after its water supply ran out on 15th February, 1956 and it was replaced by 2-6-0 No. 46437 (25G), a further unusual engine used being ex-Midland 0-6-0 No. 43308 on 3rd September, 1957. Ivatt class '2' 2-6-0s were allocated for this job but in actual fact put in their time on other duties. The Wakefield service was the first Hillhouse roster transferred to diesel operation when a 2-coach Metro-Cammell unit commenced work on 3rd March, 1958, the units being based at Bradford Hammerton Street. Initially the diesel service doubled the steam-operated service.

Dmus were not accommodated at the shed until 5th September, 1966 when four trains were housed overnight, entering from the Hillhouse No. 1 end. A big dieselisation scheme commenced on 3rd March, 1958 in a modest way with the Huddersfield-Wakefield service. The Bradford-Halifax-Clayton West and Penistone services followed in November 1959, while on 2nd January, 1961 the Trans-Pennine services commenced. Hillhouse's dwindling stud of 2-6-4 tanks eaked out their time on parcels trains to Leeds and Bradford until they too were dieselised in September 1966. Likewise the stud of 'Austerity' 2-8-0s spent their last years on local trip workings, the heaviest of which being the 'drummer' whose usual load now consisted of 24 coal wagons.

Nevertheless, occasional glimpses of past greatness became evident when a call was made for a substitute for a main line diesel failure; the shed rose to the occasion as exemplified on a bleak night in November 1956 when 'foreign' Black Stanier No. 45339 performed the not inconsiderable feat of hauling a dead English Electric class '40' and train of over 500 tons from Gledholt Jn to Liverpool (Lime Street) on only one tender tank full of water, the supply of which was restricted owing to frost.

The last men, all 99 of them, whether they were footplatemen, steam raisers, fitters or foremen shared many common characteristics. Some in their fifties and sixties were third generation railway servants; others discovered their work cut short when no longer able to conform to the strict medical standards their occupation demanded and who spent their latter years uncomplainingly on routine work inside the shed. Others found the cheerless prospect of redundancy a matter of history repeating itself. Steam had given way to diesel. Tradition takes second place to progress and a long and distinguished chapter in human and mechanical history came to an end.

A football excursion is bound for Hawthorns Halt, which served West Bromwich Albion's ground, on 19th May, 1953, hauled by Hillhouse Ivatt 2-6-0 No. 46487 and Farnley Jn 'Black Five' 4-6-0 No. 45080 passing Brook's sidings. The route of the ex-Midland Railway line from Mirfield is on the left.   *Author*

At home, Fowler '4MT' class No. 42412, 'WD' 2-8-0 No. 90325 and Hughes '5MT' 'Crab' class 2-6-0 No. 42863 on shed at Hillhouse on 16th June, 1954.   *Author*

Stanier 'Black Five' 4-6-0 No. 45069 passes Linthwaite Goods signal box with a train of flat wagons *c.* 1955. *Kenneth Field*

'WD' 2-8-0 No. 90348 passes Uppermill goods yard on the Micklehurst line between Diggle and Stalybridge on 31st August, 1957. *Author*

Queen Victoria's 12-wheel saloon in a train of similar vehicles standing alongside Hillhouse
Shed *c.* 1958.   *Kenneth Field*

Hillhouse Shed used Hughes 'Crab' 2-6-0 No. 42865 on the 2.15 pm Stockport-Bradford seen
passing Mossley on 21st March, 1859.   *Author*

BR Standard class '5' 4-6-0 No. 73165 leaving Batley on 31st October, 1959 hauling the 10.20 am Manchester Exchange to Leeds slow train. The ex-Great Northern Railway platform is on the left. The bay platform formerly used by Birstal branch trains is just visible to the right of the train. *Author*

Gresley 'V2' class 2-6-2 No. 60942 is seen on Hillhouse Shed after working a football excursion from Sunderland on 24th August, 1963. It is being hauled back and forth in the shed yard by 'Black Five' No. 45080 in an attempt to clean the fire and improve steaming. *Author*

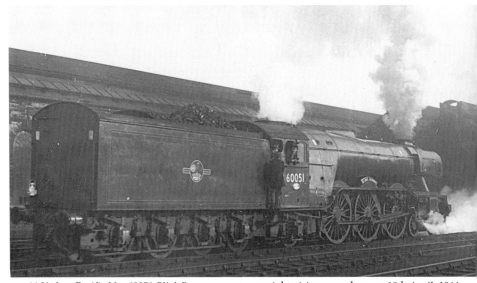

'A3' class Pacific No. 60051 *Blink Bonny* was an overnight visitor, seen here on 18th April, 1964.
Author

Ex-Great Western Railway 'Grange' class 4-6-0 No. 6858 *Woolston Grange* travelled over the
Penistone branch in August 1964, but it was by no means the first Great Western engine to be
seen at Hillhouse.   *Author*

L. S. M.
Hillhouse / R/F

BRITISH RAILWAYS
North Eastern Region

FTC (C) 16

MOVEMENTS DEPARTMENT,
REGIONAL HEADQUARTERS,
YORK

20th August, 1964

G.W. LOCOMOTIVE No. 6858 "WOOLSTON GRANGE" HILLHOUSE
M.P.D. TO OXLEY M.P.D. (WOLVERHAMPTON), WEDNESDAY,
26TH AUGUST, 1964

The above locomotive will be worked light engine under its own steam
in the following times :-

Wednesday, 26th August, 1964

		8Z02
Hillhouse M.P.D.	dep.	00.50
Hillhouse No. 1	pass.	00.55
		SL
Huddersfield	pass.	1/ 2
Gledholt	pass.	1/ 7
Marsden	pass.	1/30
Diggle Jct.	pass.	1/40

SIGNALLING

Bell signal 2-6-1 to be used throughout.

RESTRICTIONS

Must travel via Up Loop through Huddersfield Station.
"   " Up Slow line Huddersfield to Diggle Jct.
Care to be exercised when passing Huddersfield Station
Platform.
Must cross from Up Slow line at Diggle S.B. to Micklehurst
line to Stalybridge.
Stalybridge - must travel over goods lines to No. 2 Signal-
box, and must not travel through station platforms.

LOCOMEN'S WORKING

FARNLEY driver and fireman travel passenger on 1V52 22.42 Leeds -
Huddersfield, Tuesday, 25th August, and work loco. 6858 Hillhouse M.P.D.
to CREWE, return as required.

SPEED

Not to exceed 35 m.p.h.

C. BIRCH
Movements Operations Manager

'WD' '8F' class 2-8-0 No. 90680 leaves Doles Jn for Hillhouse on 27th July, 1966 in the charge of driver Harry Cole and fireman Frank Stephenson.   *Author*

The late Harry Gatenby at Hillhouse Shed in 1966.   *Author*

Running shed foreman Walter Woods, a produc of the Great Northern Railway at Bowling Jn Shee and whose great grandfather, father and tw brothers were all employed by that company Transferred to Hillhouse in 1959 and remaine until its demise.   *Autho*

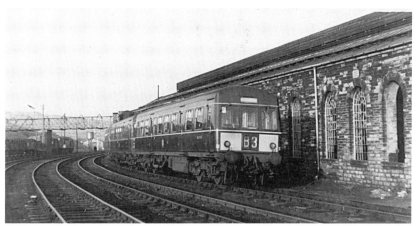

A two-coach Metro-Cammell dmu stands in Wapping siding at Hillhouse Shed.   *Author*

The allocation of steam engines was disposed of as from 2nd January, 1967 when the few remaining duties were taken over by English Electric class '40s' and the premises were downgraded to a signing-on point. Nos. D349, D352 and D398 and one brake tender arrived from Healey Mills diesel depot on 31st December, 1966 and New Year's Day. The active steam stock was disposed of: 'Austerity' 2-8-0 No. 90694 hauling 90332 to Royston; No. 90680 hauling 90649 to Normanton; No. 90363 absent at Crewe Works was turned out from that establishment on 28th December but never came back to shed. Stanier 2-8-0 No. 48540 (55D) was used by the shed until breaking a spring on 10th December and was dragged to its home depot on 31st December by Stanier 4-6-0 No. 44982. The last engine to arrive on shed was No. 90649 which had assisted BR class '9F' 2-10-0 No. 92011 on the Stanlow-Liversedge tank train. The latter proved the last engine turned off shed for the return tank train was cancelled only after No. 92011 had reached Liversedge, whereupon it ran light engine to Wakefield Shed. Two stored Fairburn 2-6-4 tanks remained for some time but on 7th April, 1967 No. 42689 was dragged to Royston and the final steam locomotive of all, No. 42141, remained until 29th of the same month when it too was towed to Low Moor Shed. Signing-on continued by the small number of men still remaining but ended on 5th November, 1967. After being used earlier in the day on ballast trains, type '4' diesels Nos. D351 and D396 moved off shed to run to Healey Mills.

Demolition took place in stages commencing on 1st January, 1968 when the roof was removed, the timber set alight and all metal recovered and track taken up. Commencing 1st May, 1968 the walls were demolished and the site levelled by the 24th. Over a year elapsed before the next work - the water tower, a 60,000 gallon structure, being felled on 18th June, 1969 followed next day by demolition of the ash plant. The coaling plant and footbridge remained until 6th July when these were taken down, the former by the use of explosives and packing the main line with sleepers for protection.

Hillhouse Shed on Christmas Day 1966.   *Author*

Fairburn '4MT' class 2-6-4T No. 42141, the last occupant of Hillhouse Shed, seen here on 11th
April, 1967.   *Author*

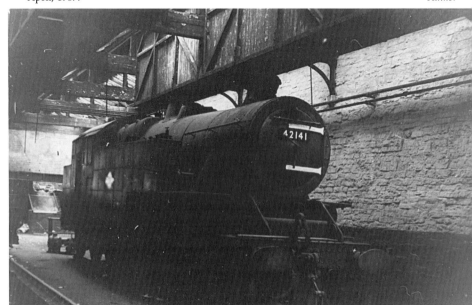

Appendix One

Summary of Engines Allocated to Hillhouse

Huddersfield and Manchester Railway and Canal Company Engines

In 1847 Sharp's supplied four 2-2-2s having driving wheels of 5 ft diameter and 15 in. x 20 in. cylinders. These bore the names *Aldam, Huddersfield, Brook*, and *Saddleworth* (*Brook* had 5 ft 6 in. wheels). The first and third names are those of William Aldam and Joseph Brook, respectively Chairman and Deputy Chairman of the company which ordered these engines. In July 1849 the first three engines were numbered 44, 45 and 46 in the engine list of the LNWR North Eastern Division. The fourth engine was transferred in July 1848 to the LNWR Southern Division, where it became number 4 by 1850.

In 1848 three Hawthorn-built 0-6-0s with 5 ft diameter driving wheels and 18 in. x 24 in. cylinders arrived, one bore the name *Standedge*. These were sent to the Southern Division where they became 246, 85A and 87A respectively. By way of exchange two old London & Birmingham ballast engines bearing the Southern Division numbers 85 and 87 were received. These were Bury 0-4-0s built in 1839 by Maudsley and Field. They were renumbered 68 and 69 in the North Eastern Division list in July 1849. Both were used in construction of the line west of Huddersfield, afterwards finding employment on the Birstal branch.

Leeds, Dewsbury & Manchester Railway Engines

Of the six 2-2-2s ordered by this company from E.B. Wilson, two were sent direct from the makers to the Eastern Counties Railway, while the remaining four were transferred in November 1847 to the LNWR Southern Division where they were numbered 201 to 204. In September 1848 Nos. 202 to 204 were sent to Hillhouse and in July 1849 received North Eastern Division numbers 40 to 42. This class had 6 ft diameter driving wheels and 15 in. x 20 in. cylinders. Six 0-6-0s with 4 ft 6 in. wheels and 16 in. x 24 in. cylinders were also ordered from E.B. Wilson and were delivered to Hillhouse, but stored from 1847 until 1849 when they were numbered 35 to 39 and 43 respectively in the North Eastern Division list.

The condition of the E.B. Wilson 2-2-2s on return from the Southern Division was very poor and after representations had been made, six outside-cylindered long-boilered 2-2-2s were obtained from the Southern Division (SD No. 191 to 196) which became 47 to 52 in the North Eastern Division list.

LNWR Engines

'Crewe Goods' 2-4-0. These were an early example of what many years later became known as 'mixed traffic engines' and used on all classes of work. By the late 1880s the last survivors ended their days as bank engines, viz. Nos. 1869, 1931, 1950 and 314. The first three were formerly named *Hurricane, Woodcock* and *Ptarmigan*. No 314 was the last of the class at Hillhouse.

Ramsbottom 'DX' 0-6-0. This class of locomotive augmented the 'Crewe Goods' on work of every description and was notable for a fine turn of speed on express workings. The class was without cab or brakes. Many of these were rebuilt as 'Special DX' 0-6-0s. Numerically the class had been thinned out by 1900 for in 1906 only Nos. 1605 and 3522 (old 560) remained. No. 1250 was outstationed at Hull in the early 1900s. Of the engines withdrawn from Hillhouse Nos. 1221, 1349 and 3275 were sold to the Malines and Ternezen Railway in Belgium.

Class 'F' class 2-8-0 No. 1273 allocated to Hillhouse in 1921-1923; this class was often enveloped in steam escaping from the front, hence being referred to as 'Swammies'.   *P.F. Cooke*

A 5 ft 6 in. 2-4-2T No. 2141 allocated between 1920 and 1923.   *P.F. Cooke*

2-4-0 tank. These were rebuilt from the 'Crewe Goods' and the old tender formed part of the engine's side tanks. No 37 was used 'on the first train to Kirkburton'.

2-4-0 saddle tank. Ahrons observed No. 232 was employed on the Kirkburton branch in 1869, while other examples were used on local passenger work at the time of the opening of the viaduct line between Farnley Jn and Leeds Canal Jn. Class rebuilt from 'Crewe Goods'.

2-4-0 tank. One of the 'Choppers' with 4 ft 3 in. driving wheels was tried out on the Kirkburton branch but proved unsuitable due to limitation in both coal and water capacity. Another of the class was used by Hillhouse men but supplied from Copley Hill for the Birstal branch.

18 in. 0-6-0 Goods 'Cauliflowers'. These Webb engines augmented and replaced the Ramsbottom 'DX' class on all manner of traffic. It was not uncommon for one to be seen at the head of an express deputising for a larger engine that had failed. In 1901/2 several new engines replaced withdrawn 'Special DXs', e.g. Nos. 451, 555, 556, 566, 879 and 2206. The final examples of the class at Hillhouse were LMS Nos. 8498/8499 and 8505 which departed Hillhouse in June 1929. From 1920 until that time no fewer than 42 had been allocated to the shed.

0-6-0 Coal Engine. A numerous engine, very occasionally seen on passenger work. The last two examples at the shed were stored there from 1931 until 1934 when LMS No. 8187 moved away. Very hard working with a pronounced barking exhaust beat.

2-4-0 'Precursor'. These were a most capable and popular engine allocated singly, Nos. 1147, 1148 and 1149, respectively *John Rennie*, *Boadicea* and *Helvellyn*, being there in the late 1880s and early 1890s.

6 ft 0 in. 'Precedent' 2-4-0. The 'Jumbos' replaced the foregoing class, No. 1220 *Belted Will* being the first followed by Nos. 1168 *Cuckoo*, 2192 *Caradoc* (in 1908) and 792 *Theorem* the last one, being displaced by a new 4-6-2 tank in 1912.

'A' class 3-cylinder Webb compound 0-8-0 goods engine. No. 1832 was the first at Hillhouse of the very small number allocated, arriving on 18th August, 1898. Nos. 1875 and 1876 appear to have been the last and moved elsewhere in 1903.

'B' class 4-cylinder Webb compound 0-8-0 goods engine. The 'Johnny Duggans' were a numerous class for many years, Nos. 1066, 1091 and 1224 being the last ones allocated, moving away in 1915.

'C' class 2-cylinder 0-8-0. This small-boilered rebuild was never plentiful at Hillhouse, No. 1844 being the last one to remain in 1918, while No. 1845 of the similar 'C1' class was at Hillhouse in the same year.

'D' class 0-8-0. The first example came in 1911 and the last, LMS Nos. 9002 and 9003, moved away in November 1930.

'G' class Superheater 0-8-0. LMS No. 9146 was the last of the 'Super Ds' being transferred in 1932, although in store prior to that.

'G1' and 'G2a' class 0-8-0. Nos. 670 and 734 were the first 'G1s' to come new from Crewe Works followed by No. 931. LMS Nos. 9381 and 9387 were the last to move away in March 1949 after the remainder of the class had been transferred, largely to the LMS Midland division in 1946.

'E' class 4-cylinder compound 2-8-0. Nos. 222 and 1223 were the most recent examples of this small-boilered class, moving away in 1915.

'F' class 4-cylinder compound 2-8-0. No. 1273 which reigned until 1923 was the last of this type, being transferred after a long period on the Birkenhead goods. Known to enginemen as 'Swammies' owing to the front end being enveloped in a cloud of steam. (The 'B' class 0-8-0s were also known by this title.)

Webb 4-cylinder compound 4-6-0 goods. Known as 'Bill Baileys' owing to their reputed failure and inability to return home, the class arrived to work the London goods. One of their other duties at that time was to work the 1.41 pm Longwood excursion to Manchester Exchange on Saturdays. No. 1113 was the last allocated, departing in 1915. Originally these engines could only be turned at Huddersfield.

Webb 4 ft 6 in. 2-4-2 tank. In 1883 eight of these arrived as the principal passenger class and reigned for more than 40 years. From 1916 motor fitted for the Kirkburton branch. Seven engines were allocated between 1920 and September 1925, when No. 825 moved away. Two of the class at Hillhouse, Nos. 2070 and 2251, were on withdrawal sold to the Dublin, Wicklow & Wexford Railway.

Webb 5 ft 6 in. 2-4-2 tank. A popular class of engine, 24 of which were at the shed from 1920 until the last one, LMS No. 6732, was scrapped in September 1929. The latter had arrived in November 1923 and was the first Hillhouse engine to be painted in the then new LMS maroon livery with large numerals on the tank sides and very smart she looked too. No. 2141 was specially allotted to work the 8.40 am Huddersfield-Stockport express.

18 in. 0-6-2 tank. These engines formed the Bulldog link. Those fitted with piston valves, Nos. 169, 189 and 2226, were regarded as better starters than those retaining slide valves. Of the 24 engines allocated from 1920 LMS No. 6891 was the last one, moving away in January 1929.

4-6-2 tank. These replaced the 6 ft 0 in. 'Precedents'. Nos. 1012 and 2670 came in 1912, giving way to Nos. 858 and 1366 with Nos. 1688 and 2669 as the last examples at Hillhouse in 1916.

19 in. Goods 4-6-0. This class was the first large engine allocated, Nos. 1996, 1997, 1998, 1999, 2003 and 2503 coming when newly built. Allocated to one driver and used on double trips and excursion work. No. 1997 was 'the daddy of them all'. In 1926 No. 2619 was dispatched for bridge testing trials on the LNER for which purpose it was fitted with a speedometer; some surprisingly high speeds were attained. From 1920-1937 engines were at different times allocated. Appropriately Nos. 1997 and 1998, by then LMS 8728 and 8729, were the last ones to move away in October 1936.

0-8-2 tank. From July 1919 when No. 1659 arrived, one of the class would always be seen at Hillhouse, usually as a bank engine to work between Heaton Lodge and Marsden. Six were allocated in total with LMS No. 7888 the final one, moving away in August 1935.

'Precursor' 4-4-0. No. 1310 *Ionic* was the only engine of this class allocated, and the first of five engines of this wheel arrangement the shed ever had.

'Renown' 4-4-0. In 1922 Nos. 1973 *Hood* and 1978 *Merlin* were specially diagrammed to work the newly-instituted Halifax-Stockport service, being outstationed at Low Moor. Both departed before the summer services of that year began. *Merlin* was notable as being the first engine turned out in the post-war period in the full LNWR livery.

Intrepid, a 'Jubilee' arrived in 1924.

'Prince of Wales' 4-6-0. Although No. 395 was the first allocated in 1921 its stay was short. In 1924 Nos. 745 *Pluto,* 1741 *Petrel,* 2442 *Odin* arrived followed in the next year by No. 1323 *Falaba.* In all 28 different 'Princes' were allocated with LMS No. 25797 the last one being transferred to Bletchley in 1937.

'Experiment' 4-6-0. For a long period in the 1920s this class was a regular performer on the Halifax-Stockport services, 17 members of the class being allocated from 1921. No. 2626 *Saracen,* allocated from 1926-28, was distinguished from others by its Belpaire firebox, superheater boiler, Eureka sight feed lubricator and was regarded as better than the remainder. LMS Nos. 5509 *Chillington* and 5511 *Banshee* were the last to remain, being in store from 1930 until 1934 and having the distinction of being the most recently-named engines allocated to the shed. From 1888 there were but 32 named engines at Hillhouse in total.

0-6-2 Coal Tank. Although a numerous class, very few found their way to Hillhouse. No. 981 arrived in June 1925 and displaced a 4 ft 6 in. 2-4-2 tank. Seven engines were present in all, LMS No. 7700 working the last train to Kirkburton on 26th July, 1930 when services were discontinued. This engine with Nos. LMS 7722 and 7752 remained at Hillhouse until September 1931 in store.

0-6-0 Special Tank. Never a prominent type at Hillhouse until the arrival of No. 3161 in June 1922, the first of eight such engines. LMS Nos. 7410, 7412 and 7417 were replaced on shunting duties by L&Y 0-6-0 saddle tanks in March 1928.

Ex-Ministry of Munitions Locomotives

MM Type 2-8-0. Fifteen of these locomotives were loaned from the ROD, but not all at once during the period from early 1920 until midnight 15th August, 1921, when they were withdrawn and placed in dumps. At that time Nos. 2849, 2861, 2912, 2927, 2935, 2962 and 2963 were allocated. Popular engines with crews.

Ex-Lancashire & Yorkshire Railway Engines

L&Y class '5' 2-4-2 tank. Engines from the numerous variations of this class displaced the LNWR 18 in. 0-6-2 tanks and 5 ft 6 in. 2-4-2 tanks, the first one, LMS No. 10694, appearing in 1927 followed by Nos. 10700 and 10841 in January 1928. No fewer than 47 of these engines were allocated. No. 10700 was held in high repute. BR Nos. 50855 and 50865 lingered on being rostered for the newly instituted Huddersfield-Wakefield express service until displaced by dmus. (Note: the term 'numerous variations' is used to cover those engines of the class distinguished in appearance by short bunker, long bunker, round top firebox, Belpaire firebox, original smokebox or extended smokebox.)

L&Y class '6' 2-4-2 tank. Eight of these superheated engines were allocated between July 1928 and April 1942. No. 10943 was the first to arrive and No. 10940 the last to go the former being considered the best of the class. The other engines were numbered 10890, 10934, 10941, 10942, 10945 and 10954.

L&Y class '23' 0-6-0 saddle tank. This class displaced the LNWR Special Tanks in January 1928, Nos. 11387, 11399, 11404, 11421 and 11433 being allocated. The final two were BR Nos. 51408 and 51524, replaced by LMS 'Jinties' in 1955.

L&Y class '27' 0-6-0. Nos. 12231, 12275, 12306 and 12433 were the first to arrive in 1928 when they took over from LNWR 'Cauliflowers' and Coal Engines. Latterly their ranks were thinned until only No. 12437 was left, this departing in December 1947. For hauling the last goods to Birstal on 16th June, 1962 BR No. 52515 was borrowed from Sowerby Bridge for the occasion, being a former Hillhouse engine.

L&Y class '28' class 0-6-0. Four of these superheated engines were at Hillhouse, LMS No. 12564 arriving in July 1926 and preceding the others by some years. (Nos. 12561, 12568 and 12606 were the others.) No. 12606 had the reputation of being a poor steamer and was the last one to remain, being withdrawn in December 1946.

Midland Railway Engines

Only four ex-Midland engines were ever allocated to Hillhouse and all were unpopular. MR 0-4-4 tank Nos. 1247 and 1277 arrived for working the Kirkburton service in November 1927, No. 1246 joining them two months later but within 10 months all had moved away. MR 0-6-0 No. 3900 was at Hillhouse for a few weeks in May 1932 .

LMS Engines

Hughes '5P4F' 2-6-0. No. 13118 had the distinction of being the first member of the 'Crabs' at Hillhouse, and also being the shed's first LMS-built engine. Twenty-three of this class were allocated in all. In June 1956 Nos. 42861, 42862 and 42863 were transferred, the only subsequent allocation being that of Nos. 42797 and 42866 for a month in 1959. The class was extensively used on double trips, excursions and is particularly recalled for their work on the 9.20 pm London goods.

Stanier 2-6-2T No. 163 after being rebuilt with a large boiler. The incident referred to opposite
occurred soon after this rebuilding.   *British Railways*

Fowler '4MT' class 2-6-4T No. 42410 stops at Batley on 5th June, 1959 while hauling the 5.50 pm
Leeds to Huddersfield train. This is the same spot where Ben Garner overshot in 1898. *Author*

Stanier '5P5F' 2-6-0. During the summer of 1934 a pair of Stanier taper boiler 2-6-0s arrived to replace 'Prince of Wales' 4-6-0s on the London goods. Some difficulty was experienced with the width over the cylinders when travelling over the Churnett Valley route. As a result their stay at Hillhouse was very brief.

Stanier '5P5F' 4-6-0. The Black Staniers arrived to replace 'Prince of Wales' 4-6-0s, Nos. 5060 and 5061 coming in April 1937 followed by No. 5062 then 5005 and 5006. No. 5061 was generally considered the finest of the 24 engines of the class allocated. In May 1953 No. 45222 was loaned to Nine Elms shed on the Southern Region where it assisted in overcoming a crisis caused by Bulleid Pacific axle flaws. The engine returned home some six weeks later with numerous additional lamp brackets adorning the smokebox door! The class was replaced by BR Standard class '5' 4-6-0s in October 1958 when Nos. 45215, 45218, 45222, 45237, 45339 and 45340 departed.

Fowler '2P' 4-4-0. From January to April 1937 LMS No. 587 was allocated, being the fifth and final example of this wheel arrangement allocated.

Stanier '3P' 2-6-2 tank. Withdrawal of L&Y 2-4-2 tanks saw the arrival of Nos. 148 and 149 in August 1937, followed a short while later by No. 160 to 164. In 1941 No. 163 was rebuilt at Derby with a '6C' large diameter boiler. When working the 7.25 pm train from Stockport to Bradford Exchange the engine broke a connecting rod while travelling at speed between Brighouse and Elland, fortunately without causing any injury. Of the eleven stationed at Hillhouse, No. 196 was the final one to be transferred away in October 1947.

Fowler '4P' 2-6-4 tank. No. 2414 preceded others of the class arriving in February 1944 for service on the Halifax-Stockport service. Its livery at the time included the small 1938-pattern numerals. No. 42384 was involved in an accident at Clayton West on 29th March, 1956, when running light it got out of control and crashed into a line of empty coaches. On 2nd November, 1959 No. 42413 was used to haul the 5.52 pm Holmfirth to Leeds City, the final passenger train to leave Holmfirth. No. 42410 survived until, as the last engine of the class, it was withdrawn on 5th September, 1966, being hauled from shed on 21st November of that year to Tipton for cutting up. This engine established a record of being the longest-lived engine at the shed, having first been allocated in March 1946.

Fowler '7F' 'G3' 0-8-0. These engines replaced ex-LNWR 0-8-0s at Hillhouse; in September 1946 Nos. 9501, 9536, 9544, 9563, 9572, 9580 and 9596 arrived. No. 9598 departed a year after the rest in May 1951, seventeen engines in all being allocated.

Stanier '8F' 2-8-0. Twelve engines were allocated but only one, No. 8106, was of LMS origin, the others Nos. 8447, 8452, 8455, 8458, 8463 and 8477 being built at Swindon, while Nos. 48708, 48714, 48715, 48726 and 48733 were constructed as LNER engines. No. 8452 was the first to arrive in April 1947 when the class augmented the 'G3s' and No. 48477 was the last to leave in December 1949.

Fairburn 2-6-4 tank class '4P'. In November 1945 Nos. 2205 to 2208 arrived new from Works, but absence of water pick-up apparatus was a hindrance and saw their replacement by Fowler engines. Nos. 42072 and 42110 were at Hillhouse for short periods while No. 42141 arrived in 1964 followed by Nos. 42689 and 42213 in 1965. The latter performed only six days work before undergoing extensive repairs after minor damage to its bunker, sustained in collision with another engine on the shed yard, and was withdrawn on 9th January, 1966.

Stanier '4P' 2-6-4 tank. Only two examples of this class were allocated, No. 42639 for a short period in 1950 and No. 42618 which came in 1964 and was withdrawn the next year.

Class '3F' 0-6-0 tank ('Jinty'). Nos. 47403 and 47556 replaced two L&Y saddle tanks in 1956 but were themselves displaced by diesel shunters in February 1958. These were the only engines allocated, although others were used on loan on occasion.

'WD' class 2-8-0 No. 90332 at Heckmondwike after working a Stanlow-Charrington Heargreaves
tanks on 17th September, 1966.   *Author*

204 hp 0-6-0 diesel-mechanical shunter No. D2263 on No. 7 road at Hillhouse when newly
allocated. This engine was tried on the Hillhouse coal chutes shunt when it pulled 80 loaded
wagons on a dry rail.   *Author*

BR Standard Locomotives

Nos. 73162 to 73166 arrived in 1958 and were never as popular as LMS Black Stanier class '5'. Several engines went for long periods on shed under repair. No. 73165 was the last one to move away in September 1964.

War Department Engines

Although WD No. 7153 was tried in July 1943 the first 'Austerity' 2-8-0s to be allocated were WD Nos. 70878 and 77205 with Southern Railway numerals and BR Nos. 90332, 90347, 90527, 90562 and 90619 within a few months. The seventy thousand series were renumbered 90335 and 90181 soon afterwards. No. 90619 was the regular engine as the Hillhouse coal chutes pilot, being equipped with a special long handled regulator. The class established something of a record for working last trains. Nos. 90308 cleared empty wagons from Birstal on 22nd June, 1962, No. 90332 worked the ultimate goods to Kirkburton on 2nd April, 1965, being followed on 9th April by No. 90347 to clear wagons. No. 90325 worked the last goods to both Meltham and Holmfirth on 2nd and 30th April, 1965 respectively.

Diesel Shunters

In February 1958 Nos. D3375, D2262 and D2263 arrived, along with D2261 sent by mistake being quickly transferred to Bradford Hammerton Street. Refuelling and maintenance was carried out at Royston Shed and the above alternated with engines from that depot as a result. No. D3375 was transferred in September 1964 when its duty as Hillhouse coal chutes pilot was abolished. No. D2262 was replaced by D2095 in 1965. No. D2263 also moved when its duty was made redundant. No. D2246 became the last engine to be allocated to the shed in September 1966, to work as Huddersfield passenger pilot engine.

Summary of Locomotives Allocated 1920-1966

4-6-0 'Prince of Wales'	28	
'Experiment'	17	
19 in. goods	37	
Stanier class '5'	24	
BR Standard class '5'	5	Total 111
4-4-0 LNWR 'Precursor'	1	
LNWR 'Renown'	2	
LNWR 'Jubilee'	1	
LMS '2P'	1	Total 5
2-6-0 Fowler '5P4F'	23	
2-6-0 Stanier '5P4F'	2	
2-6-0 Ivatt class '2'	2	Total 27
2-8-0 LNWR 'F' class	2	
2-8-0 Ministry of Munitions	15	
2-8-0 Stanier '8F'	12	
2-8-0 'Austerity' '8F'	33	Total 62

0-8-0 LNWR 'D'	23	
0-8-0 LNWR 'G1'	15	
0-8-0 LNWR 'G1' and 'G2A'	33	
0-8-0 LMS '7F' 'G3'	17	Total 88
0-6-0 LNWR Coal Engine	18	
0-6-0 LNWR 'Cauliflower'	42	
0-6-0 L&Y class '27'	17	
0-6-0 L&Y class '28'	4	
0-6-0 MR class '3F'	1	Total 82
2-6-4T Fowler	14	
2-6-4T Fairburn	9	
2-6-4T Stanier	2	Total 25
2-6-2T Stanier '3P'	11	Total 11
2-4-2T LNWR 4 ft 6 in.	7	
2-4-2T LNWR 5 ft 6 in.	24	
2-4-2T L&Y class '5'	47	
2-4-2T L&Y class '6'	8	Total 86
0-6-0ST LNWR 'Special'	8	
0-6-0ST L&Y class '23'	14	
0-6-0T LMS class 3F'	2	Total 24
0-6-2T LNWR 18 in. 5 ft 0 in.	24	
0-6-2T LNWR Coal Tank	7	Total 31
0-8-2T LNWR '6F'	6	Total 6
0-4-4T MR class '1P'	3	Total 3
Diesel Shunter 350 hp	1	
Diesel Shunter 204 hp	4	Total 5

Grand Total   566

Locomotive Allocation 2nd November, 1913

LNWR 19 in. Goods 4-6-0 Nos. 370, 392, 630, 1377, 1482, 1602, 1997, 2587, 2612
LNWR 18 in. Goods 0-6-0 Nos. 38, 64, 121, 130, 462, 475, 539, 702, 836, 1496, 1499, 2320, 2465, 2472, 2569
LNWR 17 in. Coal Engine Nos. 2096, 2368
'B' class 0-8-0 Nos. 1224, 14361, 1899, 2575
'D' class 0-8-0 Nos. 1815, 1816, 1822, 1831, 1833, 1845
'G' class 0-8-0 Nos. 1280,1464, 1789, 2566
'G1' class 0-8-0 Nos. 670, 734
'F' class 2-8-0 Nos. 906, 2573
4-6-2T Nos. 1021, 2670
5 ft 6 in. 2-4-2T Nos. 431, 779, 1165, 1463, 1758, 2131, 2217
18 in. 0-6-2T Nos. 78, 167, 188, 36, 39, 1564, 1590, 2016, 2020, 2026

Total 63 Engines

Locomotive Allocation 15th July, 1923

'Experiment' 4-6-0   No. 89   *Lady of the Lake*
                   No. 2630   *Buffalo*
                   No. 2646   *Boniface*
19 in. Goods 0-6-0 Nos. 852, 917, 1541, 2518, 2592, 2598
18 in. 0-6-0 'Cauliflower' Nos. 22, 463, 535, 777, 1027, 1641, 1724, 2329, 2331, 2333
17 in. 0-6-0 Coal Engine Nos. 1205, 3462, 3491
'D' class 0-8-0 Nos. 1804, 1830, 1832, 1863, 2551
'G' class 0-6-0 Nos. 1648, 1774
'G1' class 0-6-0 No. 859, 955, 1127, 2001
0-8-2T No. 2277
0-6-0 Special Tank Nos. 3048, 3143, 3161
4 ft 6 in. 2-4-2T Nos. 283, 384, 2515 (all motor fitted)
5 ft 6 in. 2-4-2T Nos. 187, 900, 2127, 2133, 2141, 2216
18 in. 5 ft 0 in. 0-6-2T Nos. 167, 189, 358, 377, 2026, 2113

Total 52 Engines

LMS Permanent Allocation 1926

The LMS system of permanent allocations, introduced in 1926, replaced the LNWR method of sending fresh engines from Crewe Works before calling in worn-out ones for repair. Certain classes were based on the existing allocation, i.e. motor fitted engines. Not all engines had at this time been given their LMS number, and therefore the LNWR number is also given.

Class	LMS No.	LNWR No.
'Experiment' 4-6-0	5507 *Saracen*	2624
	5508 *Buckland*	2625
	5509 *Chillington*	2626
	5510 *President Lincoln*	2627
	5511 *Banshee*	2628
	5512 *Terrier*	2629
'Prince of Wales' 4-6-0	5804-5808	357, 358, 435, 436, 438
5 ft 6 in. 2-4-2T	6730-6733	2263-2266
18 in. 0-6-2T	6860-6868	1560, 1562, 1563, 1564, 1574, 1587, 1588, 1590, 1593
'Special' 0-6-0s	7410, 7412, 7415, 7417	3255, 3374, 3544, 3590
Coal Tank 0-6-2T (motor fitted)	7679, 7680, 7700, 7752	921, 981, 3727, 3732
0-8-2T	7888	1515
Coal Engine 0-6-0	8187, 8188, 8189	3269, 3455, 3449
'Cauliflower' 0-6-0	8499-8505	1270, 1275, 2008, 2052, 2054, 2059, 2064
19 in. Goods 4-6-0	8724-8732	2029, 2044, 2173, 1996, 1997, 1998, 1999, 2000, 2421
'D' class 0-8-0	9002-9008	1866, 1845, 2548, 1822, 1863, 1873, 1874
'G' class 0-8-0	9120-9126	1070, 1385, 1449, 1492, 1507, 1539, 1577
'G1' class 0-8-0	9188-9193	2225, 2281, 2289, 2301, 2374, 328

Total 72 Engines

Locomotive Allocation 1st November, 1937

Class '6F' 0-8-0	9004, 9005, 9005, 9006, 9007, 9018, 9121, 9122, 9124, 9125, 9126, 9360
Class '4P' 'Prince of Wales'	25797
Class '2P' 2-4-2T	10694, 10705, 10719, 10729, 10755, 10765, 10809, 10822, 10870
Class '3P' 2-4-2T	10943, 10946, 10954
Class '2F' 0-6-0ST	11371, 11404, 11421, 11505
Class '3F' 0-6-0	12095, 12306, 12461, 12568
Class '3P' 2-6-2T	148, 149, 160-164
Class '5P4F' 2-6-0	2729, 2820, 2821, 2841, 2861, 2862, 2863
Class '5P5F' 4-6-0	5060-5062

Total 50 engines

Locomotive Allocation 1st December, 1947

Class '7F' 'G2a' 0-8-0	9381, 9387
Class '2F' 0-6-0ST	11408, 11447, 11524
Class '3F' 0-6-0	12351, 12437, 12515
Class '7F' 'G3' 0-8-0	9501, 9536, 9544, 9563, 9572, 9580, 9583, 9596, 9598
Class '4P' 2-6-4T	2310-2312, 2324, 2384, 2408, 2410-2414
Class '5P4F' 2-6-0	2733, 2861-2863, 2866, 2869
Class '5P5F' 4-6-0	5099, 5218, 5237, 5238
Class '8F' 2-8-0	8106, 8447, 8452, 8455, 8708, 8733

Total 44 engines

Locomotive Allocation 1st January, 1957

Class '4P' 2-6-4T	42310, 42312, 42384, 42408-42410, 42412-42414
Class '5' 4-6-0	45215, 452224 45237, 45339, 45340
Class '3F' 0-6-0	47403, 47556
Class '2P' 2-4-2T	50725, 50865
Class '8F' WD 2-8-0	90243, 90249, 90265, 90325, 90322, 90345, 90347, 90619, 90621, 90624, 90680, 90694

Total 30 engines

Locomotive Allocations 1st January, 1967

Class '4' 2-6-4T	42141, 42689
Class '8F' WD 2-8-0	90332, 90363, 90649, 90680, 90694
204 hp Diesel-Mech.	
0-6-0 Shunter	D2095, D2246

Total 9 Engines

Steam allocation dispersed 2nd January, 1967

Appendix Two

Locomotive Foremen at Hillhouse Shed

| 1847- | Mr Roach. Designated locomotive superintendent. (Sometimes referred to as Mr Rhodes.) |

1847-   Mr Roach. Designated locomotive superintendent.
            (Sometimes referred to as Mr Rhodes.)
1852-   Mr Ambrose. Later locomotive foreman at LNWR Copley Hill.
1866-   Mr Duxbury.
1870-   A. Winby. Salary £100 pa. Later locomotive foreman at Bletchley. While
            at Hillhouse was paid retainer to supervise locomotives employed at
            Blackmoorfoot Reservoir.
1873-   Christopher Marshall. Formerly assistant foreman.
1878-   Mr Blackmore.
1882-1894   Thomas Norman. Commenced at shed in 1858. Died at Oldham 1909.
1894-1911   James Goulding. Formerly at Garston. Retired and died in 1936. Son
            was driver at Bushbury.
1911-1919   Thomas Cheetwood. Formerly of Garston, later to Springs Branch then
            Longsight.
1920-1921   H.K. Bostock. Later to Bangor.
1921-1922   G.H. Nelson. Later to Carlisle.
1922-1923   W.H. Power. Later to Abergavenny.
1923-1933   W.G. Ward. (Mr Gower sub foreman).
1933-1947   Stanley Muff. Late L&Y at Low Moor. Retired.
1947-1956   G. Daykin. Later to Bank Hall.
1956-1958   G. Gant. Later to Preston.
1958-1961   B.K. Shaw.
1961-1965   N.W. Howcroft. Formerly Dairycoates, Alnmouth and Northallerton.
            Father was a NER driver.
1965-1967   C.R. Henderson. Commenced apprenticeship at Hillhouse.
            Simultaneously in charge at Manningham Shed until closure.

The Hillhouse breakdown gang on 16th September, 1907 with driver George Rolls Stocks in charge of 19 in. 4-6-0 No. 2503 with locomotive foreman James Goulding standing alongside.   *Revd R.G. Jackson*

Appendix Three

Accidents on the LNWR Yorkshire Lines 1850-1900

1850	1	1860	4	1870	11	1880	6	1890	4	1900	1
1851	2	1861	7	1871	6	1881	4	1891	-		
1852	1	1862	4	1872	3	1882	5	1892	1		
1853	1	1863	8	1873	4	1883	4	1893	2		
1854	4	1864	4	1874	-	1884	5	1894	2		
1855	-	1865	1	1875	2	1885	5	1895	4		
1856	3	1866	15	1876	2	1886	2	1896	3		
1857	3	1867	4	1877	1	1887	1	1897	-		
1858	2	1868	6	1878	3	1888	2	1898	1		
1859	-	1869	4	1879	2	1889	2	1899	1		

Total 163

Compiled from Minutes of the Huddersfield & Manchester Railway & Canal Co., LNWR (NE Division) Committee Minutes 1850-1855, ten-yearly census lists 1851-1891, *The Journal of the Stephenson Locomotive Society*, *The Railway Observer* (RCTS), and reports in the *Huddersfield Examiner, Huddersfield Chronicle, Leeds Intelligencer, Leeds Mercury, Leeds Times, Oldham Reporter, Oldham Chronicle, Ashton Reporter, Manchester Examiner* and Board of Trade Accident Reports.